Please re

To renev
or visit w

Borrowe

MY ODYSSEY

MY ODYSSEY

THROUGH WAR AND PEACE, IN AND OUT OF HOSPITAL

PHILIP A. G. KELLY

Matador
5 Weir Road
Kibworth Beauchamp
Leicester LE8 0LQ, UK
Tel: (+44) 116 279 2299
Fax: (+44) 116 279 2277
Email: books@troubador.co.uk
Web: www.troubador.co.uk/matador

ISBN 978 1848765 870

British Library Cataloguing in Publication Data.
A catalogue record for this book is available from the British Library.

Typeset in 11pt Aldine401 BT Roman by Troubador Publishing Ltd, Leicester, UK

Matador is an imprint of Troubador Publishing Ltd

FOREWORD

This book of my life was written mostly from memories that returned to me while I was slowly recovering from a mystery illness.

I had previously agreed with a few friends and well wishers some time back to write my story. With no thought of when that would be or of how it might happen. I always seemed to be too busy.

My illness whatever it was began in December 2008. The first week of that December did not register in my memory except that I can recall my medication was stopped. I began to understand that I was in some way behaving abnormally and it appeared that the medication was the cause.

By the seventh day of that month I had been visited at home by two GPs and was admitted to hospital early on the Sunday. I remained there two-and-a-half weeks but remember little of it. I know that family and church members were praying for me and some visited me while I was in hospital and later. During that month a nurse from the Ward accompanied me to a routine appointment at the ENT Clinic in Braintree.

My condition gradually improved till I was discharged from Broomfield Hospital on Christmas Eve to spend six weeks in a Residential Home in Halstead, north of Braintree. Whatever my condition may have been – some mention was made of dementia, which was in fact strongly denied by others – it definitely affected my memory. Sometimes it was improved but other times it worsened, as is normal with elderly people.

Our eldest son drove us home on 4th February 2009 but my condition remained delicate. Many long lost memories began to return from then onwards, many of them pleasurable. Being no longer young, it seemed right to use the enforced time of leisure to type my life story as it was remembered.

I trust that many readers will enjoy the following account.

Grandpa shouted. He wasn't a shouting type of person but there were times when he chose to do so. First, he shouted for help from downstairs. This would be a loud shout as it was a big house. He wanted his open coal fire drawn up because he was feeling cold. My brother David and I were the two biggest boys so we were sent up to console our grandfather. We were four brothers and we two older ones were barely suitable for Grandpa's need. The younger ones, Peter and John were quite unable for the job. Peter was then only two years old and baby John was still a few months short of his first birthday.

Grandpa was cold because it was winter and the large sash window of his bedroom was wide open. He was using one of his collection of guns, probably in this case a small shotgun, to aim at birds flying past his window. This was while sitting up in his sickbed. Firing across the room and through the open window. From time to time Granny would go outside to pick up shot birds from the snow on the front lawn. Lined up on the kitchen dresser, dead blackbirds, sparrows and other unfortunate victims lay waiting the attention of someone not ill in bed.

The job we were sent upstairs to do was to hold a sheet of newspaper across the fireplace. Very quickly, Grandpa's coal fire was blazing and he was again shouting. One corner of the newssheet had caught alight and poor David took fright. He was loudly commanded to do as I was doing and keep still. I was some fifteen months David's junior and totally in awe of the old man, quite apart from the blazing fire. I cannot recall what happened next but I guess our mother would have come to our aid. The outbreak of war was the reason we were far from home and staying with our grandparents in Lancashire.

Our Dad worked for the LNER, the London and North Eastern Railway, so he could more easily obtain fares on their lines. Our Mum was born in Preston, Lancashire where she grew up, went to school and then worked for her father's dairy. Pushing a 'pram' around Avenham district twice daily because the milk was raw, or untreated. The farmers might stand the full kits in the cattle trough as a rudimentary method of cooling. So it was to Lancashire that we youngsters were taken when the dangers of war threatened. It was late in the day when we departed our Council flat in East Ham where my brothers and I were born between late 1934 and spring 1939. Understandably, our Lancashire Lass mother was very keen to get away from Beckton Gas Works, the biggest in the world and a sure target for enemy bombs. So from the LNER Marylebone Station in the compulsory blackout, we travelled north to Manchester.

I must have slept for some of that journey. Some soldiers slept on the overhead luggage racks. Others perched on suitcases and kitbags in the corridor. Glowing cigarette-ends marked where some men were still awake. There was little else to see as the train took us north but in places I could see some coalmines as we passed them. The pithead gear always fascinated me as the spoked wheels spun in opposite directions. I knew they were not like the wheels on Dad's bike that was kept indoors at our East Ham flat. We reached Manchester eventually and from there we somehow crossed to Preston but I would be sleeping or dozing most of that time.

From Preston station we travelled out by taxicab to my grandparents home in higher Penwortham. As the rather full cab arrived at the big house, the taxi driver was asked to sound his horn. A squeeze or two of the rubber bulb brought Granny downstairs to let us in. Snow had been falling for some time and Queenie, the bullmastiff bounded out onto the snow-covered lawn. Upstairs, a flock mattress was laid over some wooden boxes – tea chests and suchlike – as a makeshift bed for us boys. Our emergency bedroom would have once been a dressing room, being between the bathroom and the landing.

Grandpa kept goats at the far end of the big orchard and we used to like going down there to see him milk them. He could not have been long in his sickbed so the local songbirds would soon have some respite. The first time we went to see the goats that snowy winter, Peter was tucked under Mum's arm, supported on her hip and I was instructed to put my small boots into her footprints. The snow may have been almost a foot deep at that time so my little feet had to be lifted quite high. We were there about six months and my eldest brother attended Penwortham village school. David's first school was in East Ham.

It would have been during this time in Penwortham that my chronic ear troubles began. I do not remember anything of that but am given to understand that it was a worrying time. The Family Doctor was a lady who was extremely concerned for my health. She was making twice-daily visits for my care. Although I remember nothing of it, the story of my life would be incomplete without some mention of it. My mother's father, a retired businessman, would have paid the doctors bills. Another five years would pass before my ears required emergency surgery.

Grandpa's first shop had been in Stanley Street, Preston, for his Jewellery business after he completed his apprenticeship to a German Watchmaker and Jeweller. To keep body and soul together he took a clerking job for the Army at Fulwood Barracks and later he drove the new electric trams. His second shop for the Watchmakers and Jewellery business was on the corner of Bow Lane and it was from there that the dairy began. A summer drought when low milk yields made it unprofitable for farmers to sell milk in towns caused my grandfather to start dairying. After seeing mothers of infants jug in hand on street corners he began collecting milk from farms to sell in town.

At first with a single kit (churn) on a trade carrier bicycle my maternal grandfather soon found the need growing. Long before my own lifetime, the diligence of his younger days always interested me. His attention to the needs of others soon led him to employ a man with a horse. Later, he had a Ford van and driver. The Model 'T' van served well and Grandpa was soon driving it himself. My Uncle Jack was driving it in Fulwood in freezing fog once with my mother beside him when they crashed. This left her with fragments of windscreen glass in her hand. Grandpa's many exploits might make another book but this is my story.

Subsequent holidays were enjoyed at "Bloomfield". The country house and large orchard had so much to take our interest. Quite apart from the working farm across the road where we could watch the farmer milk his cows by hand, we might see Grandpa milk his goats and help sort the fruit. The house itself was like an old curiosity shop. I remember an old Yew longbow, an Assegai, a knobkerrie and the sword bought for my mother's eldest brother when he became an Army officer. But most memorable were the numerous clocks everywhere of many types and the gun collection from which we boys were kept distant. Grandpa's old wildfowling punt gun seemed to us like a cannon. The one gun we used under strict supervision was a 22-calibre shotgun, which had been borrowed and part of its stock sawn off.

Throughout the war, my father worked shifts at Bishopsgate goods station in the East End of London. I do not remember how often he visited us in Lancashire but I do know snowdrifts blocked the main railway line at one time. With no trains running on the main line, Dad was unable to reach his job but he walked every day to Penwortham station to know when the trains were running again. In later years we used that wayside station with its wooden platforms for occasional trips to Southport. That was when we spent holidays with our grandparents' at Penwortham and with other family members in Preston. Our wartime situation with our Dad's job 200 or so miles from most of his family was far from ideal.

Being churchgoing Christians, my parents would have been praying for God to supply their great need. The answer came through one of my father's cousins in Essex. In the 1930s the Ministry of Transport were planning to construct a bypass of Ingatestone village. In preparation for this the Ministry had bought a row of eight houses between the Boys School and the Girls and Mixed Infants. The row comprised a terrace of six gabled Victorian cottages and a more modern semi detached pair. To obtain a lease of one cottage, Dad took his first opportunity to visit the Estate Agent.

He took me with him by train to Ingatestone with his trusty Co-op bike to ride to Ingleton's office near the parish church. I rode on his rear carrier. Being possibly four years old by then, I should have been safe but one or perhaps two of my fingers became trapped in Dad's saddle springs. We were in the High Street (Roman Road) near the Alms Houses and Dad was not pleased at having his important journey interrupted. We arrived at Ingleton's office without further mishap and Dad was able to secure the lease of one of the Victorian cottages.

When we left East Ham to move into our new home, we boys were suffering from some childhood malady and I do not remember the journey out. Without a stick of furniture, we sat on the wooden stairs until the van arrived. There was little traffic on the roads in those days and we boys were soon running outside to welcome the van arriving with our belongings. As the bulky vehicle turned off Fryerning Lane into New Cottages road,

Uncle Tom, who was sitting on the tailboard covered in dog hairs, dropped Tim the dog off to run behind for the final few yards. My impression was that this was how the twenty miles or so had been covered and I shouted such to Peter. I believe Tim was a good dog but he could never run twenty miles.

As soon as the beds had been put up, we were tucked in to recover from the measles or whatever we had. I remember watching the gas fitter putting a gas lamp on the side of the chimneybreast in our room. Each room had a gas lamp installed but the smallest bedroom had no fireplace so therefore no chimneybreast. Both double bedrooms had an open fireplace. Downstairs we had a sizeable front living room and this had a gas lamp in the centre of the ceiling. The kitchen/scullery had not only a light but also a supply to the cooker. Later, we had a gas boiler for laundry and bathing. The galvanised bath was laid on Hessian sacks to keep it from the cold quarry-tiled floor.

The gas stove from the Gas Light and Coke Company served us well for many years for most of our meals. We had a solid fuel kitchen stove in the front room but little cooking could be done on that. Its big oven hardly got hot enough for cooking but Mum sometimes used it to warm clothes. And we warmed bricks in it for warming the bed. One time I well remember. We arrived home to find a smell of scorching clothes and Mum was almost beside herself as she raked the oven contents into a galvanised bath. Quickly taking the bath of clothes into the backyard she laid a doormat over it to exclude the air. I'm sure some were salvageable. I have rarely seen my mother so upset — and she had a vicious temper as we all knew.

Shortly after we moved into Number 3 at "New Cottages" as our Victorian terrace was named, my older brother David and I were exploring the local district. Possibly our first time in what became known as Pemberton Avenue was suddenly interrupted by machine-gun fire. Far above our heads were four aircraft shooting at each other. This unmistakeable introduction of war brought our youngest Step-sister Kathleen hurrying to conduct us home. I later became interested in all types of aircraft but those four were most likely Hawker Hurricanes and Messerschmitt 109s. I was then no older than four years but the Battle of Britain had begun.

Each of the Victorian "New Cottages" had a brick-built shed with a tiled roof. The place was infested with rats that could not be kept out of the shed with potatoes stacked inside. We had half-ton loads of potatoes delivered from a Highwood farm. Dad nailed a piece of a galvanised bath across the hole gnawed by rats at the bottom of the shed door. And the Council rat-catcher had little or no success. Trapping did nothing to diminish the rat population. The answer to the problem came from friends in Kent. We travelled there by bus to Tilbury and the Ferry to Gravesend. Mother's friends in north Kent allowed us the pick from a litter of kittens and Mum chose a pretty tortoiseshell female. She matured into all we needed and more. Far more.

The shed had a cement floor and Dad's bike no longer had to take up living space indoors. Years later I learned that he bought the bike about the time of my birth. Granny Kelly (Mrs Gladwin) had died around that time but she would have had nothing to leave her eldest son. That bicycle came new from the Co-op and I believe Dad paid all of £2 for it. His railway pay in 1936 would be no more than £2 weekly so he paid for his bike at a shilling per week.

I remember when, in East Ham he came home one day with a Bakelite visor fitted to the front lamp for the blackout. And my little fingers soon snapped off part of the new visor. Another time I remember seeing my father cycle home with a moses-basket crib for the new baby. It was on his back and fitted over his head like a too-small sentry box. Dad must have been on his 6 am to 2 pm shift when John was born. By then David had started school, leaving just Peter and me to be kept away from Mum and the new baby. It was a torment to be kept from seeing our mother.

My fingers were still inquisitive some years later when we lived in Ingatestone. A policeman once told dad that his rear lamp was too bright. Finding a pot of red paint in use somewhere, he painted a coat on the lamp glass. Feeling quite pleased with his handiwork, Dad was keen to show us the shiny red paint. The curving scratch made by my fingernail could be seen throughout the remaining years of the war. All that time he was cycling to the station for his train to London. Few trains then stopped at Ingatestone and my father quite often cycled to Brentwood station. Or Brentwood and Warley as it was then known.

Working a three-shift system to keep Bishopsgate goods station going round the clock would often mean Dad riding his bike in the dark. A policeman once diverted him from Shenfield Road because of an unexploded bomb. So, on a road he didn't know, he had to find his way to Brentwood station in the blackout. My brothers and I found the war familiar and entertaining. We watched fortifications such as tank traps being constructed around us. Concrete dragons teeth we called "pimples" were built between our cottages and the Pemberton Avenue council houses. Wooden formers shaped the concrete cones, which we later played on. At least once I watched the night time sky with stabbing searchlights and red tracer shells.

A dding to his experience of schools in East Ham and Penwortham, David began at his third school, the Girls and Mixed Infants in Fryerning Lane. Soon it was my turn to start there. Mrs Simmons, our Teacher, walked from her home in The Meads past New Cottages road each day. When one morning she had to pass workmen using noisy pneumatic drills, I was far too fascinated by this new experience to notice our teacher pass by. It was only when one of the workmen directed me to see her waving at me that I thought of school and ran there.

O ther workmen built brick air-raid shelters with flat concrete tops in the playground. The pneumatic drills were for installing rows of sockets across the road and the sockets were for placing portable anti-tank barriers. These were 'H' girders welded into giant vees. I often tried to imagine how these might appear in use but they were never used. Britain was then a mainly Christian country and we were spared the enemy invasion experienced by other countries. It was no easy matter but the men and aircraft of the RAF were able to maintain the required air superiority.

T he various defences would be intended to delay an enemy because gun emplacements were installed nearby. We watched two soldiers dig a slit trench close to the road and line it with sandbags. Within a couple of days the trench was filled in and a bigger gun position was constructed on a mound perhaps 30 or 40 yards off. One day the local Home Guard filled other gaps with rolls of vicious barbed wire. Telephone wires were laid across the intervening fields to link their Drill Hall to the lookout post on the tower of Fryerning Church,

R ex Nottage was ready to mark my first day at school. He was older and obviously knew more than me. We attended the same Sunday school and became friends in later years. But that first morning, Rex took advantage of my naïvety encouraging me to run quickly around the playground perimeter until a tree would grow from the top of my head! He was perhaps a year older than I was and may have been caught by this trick on his first day. But before the halfway point, the teacher came out to ring the hand-bell for Assembly. The bell saved me! Assembly was held in the Girls School and we little ones used to file through to stand along the front. It was there that I saw a film for the first time. Two short films in fact. One was a film from the war – Sink the Bismarck or some similar Newsreel – and the other a comedy.

Watching a film will frequently exercise my powers of comprehension and this was so that first time. Filming an aircraft as it hurtled along the runway towards the camera and its immediate departure away from the camera was beyond my understanding. The heavy bomber appeared to pirouette and to continue its journey by 180 degrees. I felt sure this was impossible for such an obviously heavy object. And I was no better at understanding the comedy film. This involved a common red pillar-box occupied by someone who was able to walk around while remaining invisible inside. It was obviously intended to confuse people in the street and it certainly confused me.

Some parts of our early school days were quite enjoyable. Getting to know others from Ingatestone village and the surrounding countryside was interesting. From Mill Green came the Meadows boys, Alan and Peter, who were sometimes brought by an older sister. Otherwise they were not in class. And even then they preferred to sleep. They lived in the woods and most likely never had a regular bedtime. I soon made friends with Bill and Bob Warren, twins from the Beggar Hill community. Also from there were Jack Vince, Mick Harvey and his sister and the Stains boys.

Derek Palmer may not have had the advantage of living next to Mrs Simmons in The Meads as did John Shepherd but Derek always seemed special. He was the only one I ever remember catching our respected teacher with an April fool joke. At 5 years of age, Derek seemed to have self-confidence that I lacked. Many years later at Secondary School, when a new Headmaster decided we should have a Head Boy, Derek was an obvious and popular choice. Later still, Derek volunteered to coach me in running for the Mid-Essex Sports. I was pleased to think that in height and weight I then equalled Roger Bannister, although I did not join in the Sports Day. Leaving Ingatestone for Brentwood had unsettled me. The plans for a By-pass of Ingatestone village had been revived and accordingly my mother eventually bought a terrace cottage in Brentwood. "Rose Cottage" in Alfred Road.

As my brothers and I were growing up, we were each in turn treated to a Saturday with our dad at his job. For myself I enjoyed the individual attention and care which could never happen when we went anywhere as a family. First we had a packed lunch of sandwiches with a choice of fillings. One special and rare choice was cheese with jam. Travelling up to Liverpool Street on the train with dad was part of the adventure. Inside the enormous Bishopsgate Goods Station was quite dark and gloomy. It was good to have our big strong father to walk beside.

He worked as a Capstanman on the upper level where daylight could reach. The electric capstan was generally used to pull a single wagon from the hydraulically powered hoist. There were occasional times when Dad would have to move a train of many wagons. A new rope would be coiled close by when the rope in use was wearing thin. A breaking rope could go like a gunshot with great force. Stirring the many pigeons into alarmed flight. I remember Dad clapping his hands to make them fly. He once lifted me up to point out to me the dome of St Paul's Cathedral

Chronic ill health may have prevented me from becoming an athlete and I was forbidden to swim. But I was once commended for my ability at cross-country running by Peter Finch. I understood he was the Head Boy at the King Edward VI Grammar School in Chelmsford. In fact, he advised me to let him run on while I waited for my brother David to catch up. We were then in the middle of one of Major Upton's woods as we followed the foxhounds. By the time David came along, I was lonely, feeling frightened and lost.

Following the hunt is both excellent exercise and a time honoured country custom. Most times, we did no more than attend the Meet wherever it happened to be. When the hunt met at the Green Man at Edney Common, we could follow on foot after leaving our bikes with family somewhere. At least once the meet was at Ingatestone Hall. That was when my father pocketed a half-crown for holding a gentleman's horse. Every Boxing Day when the hunt traditionally met at the Leather Bottle, Blackmore, we would cycle there as a family. Afterwards, we might ride on to see my father's relatives Will and Hilda Oddy along the Highwood road.

My three close brothers would have created in me a competitive advantage over Derek Palmer. He and I were quite parallel as we progressed at learning to read. Mrs Simmons would give the class a passage to learn and we each would return to her knee and demonstrate our progress. Derek and I learned rapidly and were soon well ahead of our classmates. I don't suppose he thought any more about it than I did – I just enjoyed learning and I'm sure Derek did too. But it was in Scripture lessons that my companion was not Derek but my younger brother Peter. We both earned Certificates for Scripture knowledge, which were presented to us by Mr Turner, the Head at the Fryerning Lane Boys School.

In the mercy and foreknowledge of God, I was soon to be separated from the others. They would move on to their next school, Girls or Boys, after reaching the age of seven years. But I had moved when only six! The school heads apparently had conferred and the decision was taken to make a place for one boy to move on from Infants to Boys a year early. The two candidates were obviously Derek and I. No one, child, teacher or parent, could have guessed that my schooling in the usual way would soon be ended. But I was the one selected and spent a year with older boys in History and suchlike away from the infants' class. I wonder what Derek thought of this or if it ever crossed his mind?

Those History lessons were merely stories from the childhood of men who later became important. Admiral Nelson for instance, as a boy crossed a field to visit his grandmother. The field contained a bull but the boy Nelson knew no fear. Another boy climbed a church tower before he became famous for something in India. These stories were perhaps meant as an introduction to events we might encounter in subsequent education. But for me, they were all I would get while in school. Only after retiring from full time work, I managed to earn a few 'O' levels including Modern History, starting from 1795.

Our Teacher in the 1940's was Miss Todd who played the piano for hymns at Assembly. I enjoyed singing and in music lessons Miss Todd used to get me to help. She would ask me to face the other boys and sing scales and new songs. I thought nothing of going up and down Doh Ray Me Fah So Lah Tee Doh tee lah so fah me ray doh. At church and in Sunday school I joined in all the singing and enjoyed it all. No one ever remarked on it or – quite rightly – appeared to notice me. But before too long that was to change.

This was still wartime and many boys had fathers away in the fighting forces. They may have been more likely to truant than we with fathers at home. But in summer 1944, I was presented with a special prize for being the only pupil with a perfect attendance record. Not as much as a half-day absent. Mother said the prize should be hers for sending us. No rejoicing or congratulations at my honour. I still have that prize, a book, "The Paper Boat" by Edgar Primrose Dickie. Then just a few months later, I was rushed to hospital, fevered with double mastoiditis.

Our family doctor, Dr Steen, recognised my symptoms immediately because his daughter once had the same. With no telephone available, Dad hurried down to get the one taxi driver in the village, Jack Shuttleworth. The other taxi owner, Jim Westle, like many other villagers, was away to the war effort. Arriving at the Chelmsford & Essex hospital, Jack was asked to carry me inside the front entrance. He told me some years later his arms were almost pulled out but six weeks later after no physical activity and major surgery, my weight was much less. A bed was ready for me in a first-floor room and my father had to carry me upstairs in his arms. Dr Steen would have phoned ahead for my admission.

Unfortunately, there was no Ear, Nose and Throat surgeon there at that time. Knowing they would be sent for if my very low condition deteriorated further, my parents had to leave me with the assurance they would come back if they could. Child patients were not allowed visitors. My only comfort was the sight of a single barrage balloon waving at the end of its tethering line. The balloon was strategically placed at Widford where the main A12 trunk road crossed the East Coast line of the LNER. Watching that balloon may have preserved my sanity. Not long after, I was taken downstairs to a waiting ambulance. A continuing problem was that I was continually left without any explanation of anything.

Where were they taking me? What was being done? And when would life return to normal? These were constant thoughts and fears. The ambulance was to convey me to Colchester for surgery that was unavailable at Chelmsford. Fear of the unknown was constantly with me day and night. In the 'tilly' type ambulance with me, I had a pleasant middle-aged female attendant. The driver was a man. As an eight-year-old schoolboy, to be hurrying somewhere by road was far more preferable to being alone in a strange room and bed. As we hurried towards Colchester, a crashing clatter aroused me from slumber. My stretcher was behind the driver and the attendant was sitting on the nearside facing me.

The sudden clatter was caused by the collapse of the upper ladder-type support over the attendant's head. Those little ambulances could contain a total of four stretchers. Two were low with two above. The straps had worked loose and the attendant's head was poking through the "ladder" which lay around her head and over her shoulders. The driver stopped and quickly came to release his crewmember. Both showed some amusement but he checked the ladder straps above me just in case. I did my best to hide when some home-going schoolboys looked at me over the tailboard. Before long we resumed our emergency journey to the Essex County Hospital in Lexden Road, Colchester, for what was a nightmarish experience. Had I not been so ill, I would have enjoyed that ride in a military type vehicle. My brothers would surely have been envious.

Before being allocated to a bed in a Ward, my head had to be shaved in preparation for surgery. An unfortunate Porter had to do this and I felt grateful to the accompanying nurse who offered her sharp scissors to make his work a little easier. Every nurse then had a pair of sharp scissors. Now we have 'Health and Safety' and sharp objects must be kept beyond reach. My fevered head was badly swollen. One doctor remarked later that I had a "face like a full moon". Shaving such a swelling I imagine would be like shaving a balloon or an overripe peach. Being so ill, I could barely take in what was happening. It would be night time when I was in surgery. The events of that time haunted me for years but I will spare the reader any details. It was a half-waking nightmare when I must have been close to death's door. Suffice to say that for years afterwards I feared to pass within sight of a hospital.

Some brighter interludes cheered me. Miss Todd thoughtfully gave the whole class the task of writing to me. I was interested to read that assortment of letters, unmarked and posted in a single envelope. Some were serious, others jocular, but all showed individuality and I kept them for years. Another bright spot came when two single-engine monoplane fighters roared past at a very low level. "Spitfires", I yelled to Richard Skinner in the next bed. Probably they would in fact be Mustangs from Wormingford. Richard was a boy from Brightlingsea of similar age to me. His mother brought him delicious homemade cheese sticks, which he was happy to share.

This was not a children's Ward and I was fortunate to be alongside Richard Skinner. On the other side of my bed was an elderly woman who may have been too unwell to notice us youngsters. I remember a girl not far away in that long Ward. She was twelve years old whereas us two boys would be eight years. The Ward had three large Tortoise stoves for space heating and Porters fed two of them occasionally with hods of coke. When a little boy of five years was brought in, the nurses – wearing 3 or 4 different types of cap or bonnet – expected me to take an interest in him. But Michael was at the further end of the Ward, almost too far away to be seen.

They seemed to hope I might know little Michael because like me he was from Ingatestone. He yelled and screamed in terror when he had to be x-rayed. Again, it was the problem of no careful explanations. In 1944 with a war on, x-ray equipment was both noisy and primitive. The massive machine in bright metal and cream enamel was wheeled into the Ward to Michael's bed. His fear seemed to fill the Ward. Perhaps I slept, as I remember nothing more of that. But I clearly remember one time when a number of doctors were around my bed and a chloroform pad was pressed hard over my nose and mouth. A dreadful experience for an eight-year-old. That may have been when they discovered an abscess in the wound.

My fear increased whenever my bed was made up with heavy sheets through which poles were inserted to convey me away somewhere. I may have undergone a further operation that week. We know only that a nurse informed my mother, "Did you know that you almost lost him"? Whatever the facts may have been, I am certain that I came as close to death's door as it is possible to be and survive on earth. A quite ghastly experience but I am sure God kept me in the land of the living for His own purposes.

After six weeks bedridden, my parents came to take me home. We met the train at Colchester North Station. St Botolphs station would remain closed for the duration of the war. With insufficient trains running, every seat was taken, many of the large number of passengers being military. Undaunted, my father requested the guard to permit us to journey homeward in the luggage van. Being without the use of my legs, I made the ride lying across a pile of lumpy mailbags. From the train I finished the journey on my father's shoulders. I do not know how many boys then attended our school but most of them lined the railings as we passed. Until my hair re-grew I wore a warm hood or a knitted balaclava.

Following two or three major operations, return visits to see the Consultant at the Outpatient's Department were required. To begin with, I went by train with my mother to Colchester. Very little would have changed in the hospital since Victorian times. Uniforms, equipment, treatment, even the paintwork and furniture were all quite depressing. The permanganate of potash mouthwash we were given and tow for toilet use seemed very harsh. On one train home, we shared a compartment with some American servicemen – a delightful interlude and a break from the widespread depression. One of them offered us some of the chewing gum that all children desired in those times. Mum refused but I was happy to have a piece.

My brothers would have envied me – although with a knitted hood to cover my still almost hairless head, the Americans mistook me for a girl. My subsequent Outpatient's appointments were at the Chelmsford & Essex hospital where we could go by bus. I remember little of those visits but vividly recall the strong army presence along the route. Most of the bus route followed the A12 and the southern side of the pre-war dual carriageway between Widford and the Three-mile-hill was for a time given over to the army. Soldiers with vehicles of many types were camped along that road and all traffic had to use the Hylands side.

Sharing life with my brothers, I soon regained the use of my legs. We roamed nearby farmland, allotments and waste ground that had been a tip prior to the outbreak of war. Like similar tips, the superabundance of nitrogen resulted in a plentiful growth of stinging nettles. A stream crossed this ground fed from a nearby spring-fed pond. Our neighbour Lionel Stiff the postman, used to keep ducks there. Not far from that stream – a tributary of the river

Wid – we discovered a colony of Great Crested Newts. Unfortunately for them, our cat Ginny who followed us children everywhere proceeded to consume the whole colony over the ensuing weeks. Not satisfied with rats, mice, voles and rabbits, she would eat frogs and whatever else she could find. Excepting shrews, which are distasteful to cats.

Eventually, I was able to return to school but poor Miss Todd was disappointed that I could no longer sing. With both my eardrums and the tiny bones of hearing removed along with much else, I could hear very little. The war was not yet won and no remedial education was then available. While I continued to attend school, I had to spend the time reading at the back of class. "Children of the New Forest" was a book I loved. Another, more up to date, brought the possibilities of long distance radio to my notice. I do not remember the book's title but it told of a frame aerial on the roof of a house, by which a message from South America was detected. Thus began an Intercontinental expedition and adventure of travel by land yacht with piranhas and much more.

I knew little of radio then but I had already become interested in gardening. My father spent hours on our garden and his allotment, growing food to feed us all. He also grew vegetables on the next-door plot, besides jobbing gardening for some of the big houses in Fryerning. He brought me an old lantern cloche from The Bays, by the Woolpack. I treasured that piece of Victoriana even with some of its panes missing. At school we were each encouraged to have a small plot and I was awarded a prize or two for mine, One shilling and also a second-hand copy of the Jules Verne novel "Twenty Thousand Leagues Under The Sea".

One memory from my childhood was a road traffic accident involving a horse. A group of us came across a horse and two-wheeled tumbrel with the horse suspended high by the collar. A piece of the harness had broken and the cartload of timber had tipped backwards, lifting shafts and the forelegs of the horse above ground level. The horse was gasping for air and his driver, Herbie Camp – brother of George Camp the village cobbler – seemed too distressed to take action. Just then the Prudential Agent Mr Worricker arrived and asked Mr Camp how he could help. Quickly taking a pickaxe handle on the carter's instructions, he hammered out the heavy bar across the shafts and we were all relieved to see the horse with all four feet on the ground.

Remembering my first attempt at helping my elders and betters, when Grandpa was ill in bed, some readers may expect to hear more about our contacts with my mother's father. He once cut some stout and straight sticks from a privet hedge. He stripped the bark from them and took trouble to carefully smooth them with the edge of a broken windowpane. I do not remember what he used for string but we were happy with our longbows, which we took with us home to Essex. Grandpa once explained to me how I could repair a broken mainspring of a Hornby clockwork locomotive. And when visiting our home in Ingatestone, the old man liked to walk down to watch the traffic passing through the High Street.

Following our eleventh birthday, we had to move on to Secondary School. Girls and boys together were bussed to Moulsham Secondary Modern Girls and Boys Schools. The two schools were built around a grassed quadrangle with a library at the front and gymnasium at the back. Both schools used these at different times. We were approximately six hundred boys whereas the school was built for merely four hundred. Extra classrooms and craft rooms had been added but of course the Hall could not be enlarged. Standing close together for Assembly, it was normal for one or two boys to faint from lack of oxygen. Teachers standing by the doors open to the quad were the only ones fortunate to have fresh air. Just once I was taken away before I fainted but I was sometimes absent for whole weeks or months after surgery.

At first, we were allocated to classes according to our reports from the village schools. Besides Ingatestone, we were from Margaretting, Galleywood, Widford, Sandon and Great Baddow. Having little formal education after the age of eight, I was assigned to sit in Class 1c and was dismayed to find some of my new classmates had been in that same class the previous year. One or two had still not learned to read! With the difficulty of my lack of hearing, I was quickly moved to a desk in the front row from being at the back with dunces.

To assess our abilities better, we were given tests and I was determined to do my best. But some of the boys merely wanted to play around and in my opinion, to waste time. After three years stagnating, I was keen to learn all I could. With oral questions, I was of course at a distinct disadvantage but I was quite experienced in guesswork. Wrong guesses can cause embarrassment.

Before too long I found myself moved to the B stream but with the next younger age group. So when my brother Peter passed his eleventh birthday to start at Moulsham, I was put in his class.

In the B-stream, we had lessons previously unheard of, music, science, geometry, literature and algebra. I always had to sit in the front row to be able to understand the teacher better while Peter could be at the back and not try so hard. This was the situation in music lessons. Peter in the back row would happily chat with Jack Hart. Unconcerned that they were frustrating the teacher, besides those of us keen to absorb all there was time for. I felt sorry for our teacher perhaps more than for myself. I coped easily with the treble clef, EGBDF and FACE. Being young, I assumed there would be time later to master the Bass clef, and the key and time signatures.

But this was not to happen. In my second year at Moulsham, I was once again struck down by double mastoiditis. The fever was just as severe as before and my head again had to be shaved. Only this time there was an experienced ENT surgeon at Chelmsford & Essex hospital. So I was admitted there under Mr Henry. Now aged twelve, I was able to take more notice of my surroundings and events. The 'A' Ward for men's surgical was overcrowded and I had one of a row of beds up the Ward centre, where the tortoise stoves had stood at Colchester.

Later I had a bed at the side of the Ward and was there for Matron's daily rounds. As with the doctors, I had no idea of what she might be saying to me. When Matron's visit was due each morning, white counterpanes were unfolded and spread over all the beds. Thereby concealing the usual red blankets. After Matron had gone elsewhere, the counterpanes were refolded and returned to store. This was at the inauguration of the NHS and many changes were being introduced. One was the departure of Mr Henry and his dog. He was not happy having the Government as his employer.

A week or two after my drastic surgery, I was moved to the Bellfields Annex. This was far better for a youngster. Still sharing with older men and still confined to bed. With the busy New London Road in front there was plenty to hold my interest. Later I was moved again to a bed in a back room where I could see trains crossing the Chelmer Viaduct. One dark night a spectacular thunderstorm illuminated the Viaduct from behind. Outside the window was a tennis lawn where, during daylight hours, I might see nurses practising. The day the visiting doctor decided I had recovered sufficiently to be allowed out of bed, I was the last to know.

The other patients could hear what nurses and doctors said but no one seemed to notice my deafness. But that is the nature of this common difficulty. Being able to walk and to sit outside for fresh air greatly enhanced my return to health. Besides the tennis lawn at the rear of Bellfields House there were gardens with some old apple trees. At the furthest reach was a wall beyond which was Essex County Cricket Ground. One afternoon I looked over the wall to see Mr Fred Porter who taught Metalwork at Moulsham Senior Boys School. With his pipe in his mouth, he glanced up to see me looking over the wall. He didn't speak and I felt too shy to say anything.

Letters and postcards were a genuine joy but an almost daily pleasure were the visits of my step-sister Ivy. She worked at the Crompton Parkinson Factory and cycled between the Factory and her lodgings. Almost daily she would go out of her way to see and wave to me standing at the entrance to Bellfields. Ivy had also been my most frequent visitor in 1944 at Colchester. It was fortunate for me that I was never on a Children's Ward where visiting was not permitted. A Mixed Ward in Colchester and a Men's Ward in Chelmsford allowed me the benefit of regular visiting times.

Six weeks in hospital for a second time and continuing deafness prevented any possibility of general education. While unfit to return to Moulsham I was blessed to stay with my aunt at Loves Green. My father's sister Elsie was very gentle, kind and caring. But as soon as I was deemed fit enough, I rejoined my brothers and the others on the Ashdowns bus to and from Moulsham. Activities outside school interested me as much as lessons. Peters & Barham had a large gravel pit just to the west of the school railings. I was fascinated by the action of a dragline excavator from which dumpers distributed gravel elsewhere around the site prior to its closure.

I could always find something to take my interest. Besides the gravel pit alongside the school, Curry's potato field at the back from time to time had a large flock of lapwings on it. Or there might be farm cultivations to watch. Then there were our lunchtime jaunts. We Ingatestoneites might take a packed lunch and we often walked to Oaklands Park with its many trees, swings, slide and roundabout and not least the county museum. Builders working at the school could also take our interest. It was not long before a new wall topped by a tubular rail was wrecked. The Foreman asked the Head teacher if their lorry had damaged it.

Jock Hutchinson, our much loved Head, knew his boys. "No," he replied. "That was our Wild Men of the Woods." Meaning the Sam Meadows boys who loved climbing and swinging hand over hand. School continued but before another year was over, I was hospitalised yet again. Following the double mastoids at ages 8 and 12 years, at age 13 years the infection struck only my right ear. So only that side of my head required shaving. But the illness seemed just as bad. By then though, penicillin was available. Frequent doses of the antibiotic with a large needle left my rear dotted with small scabs.

I much preferred to have the injections in my behind that was soft after weeks in bed. When nurses came to find me sitting in the garden where I was sent, they would put the large needle into a thigh muscle, which would be tense in anticipation. This was always a very unpleasant sensation. We could see the cricket ground no longer since new buildings filled the lower part of the gardens. Many years later, the man who led the haematology department there told me other staff would come to sit on his benches to watch the cricket. I was in hospital only four weeks that time but still had a long period of convalescence either at home or with Auntie Elsie.

When Mr Henry, the ENT Consultant who retired in 1948 at the start of the National Health Service, operated on my left ear, he opened a permanent fistula behind the ear. My mother was instructed to obtain a fine-point ear syringe and to irrigate the ear with warm Dettol solution. I had to hold a small kidney bowl to catch the solution as it ran from the natural ear canal. This daily chore was unpleasant for both of us but it may have averted further surgery on that ear. Thank God it did not become a lifetime duty as someone suggested. Any hint of infection since then is promptly treated with antibiotics. And nowadays ears such as mine are always to be kept dry.

Family holidays were always a welcome break from routine. Always travelling by train – sometimes for a day by the sea, most often at Walton-on-the-Naze – and a few times each year for a week or so further from home. These longer times would be with Mother's relatives in Lancashire or otherwise with my step-sister Dorothy, my father's eldest daughter, who lived within walking distance of the New Forest. At both of these, in Lancashire and in Hampshire, Dad would have a neglected lawn to scythe. Tents for us boys were sent by train to Romsey and we slept two boys in each tent on the front lawn. Forest ponies sometimes strayed into the garden and I remember a group of them being chased by a farmer on horseback. Straw from a nearby farm helped to insulate us from the hard ground.

Our holidays and the rail journeys north to Preston or south to Hampshire added greatly to my knowledge of geography, history and general knowledge. Trains between Euston and Preston did not always use the same route or stop at the same stations and these variations added to the interest and to my education. Likewise our journeys between Waterloo and Southampton stations sometimes differed. Passing the famous Brooklands banking, it was shocking to see trees growing through the concreting. Nearing Southampton we passed the airport at Swaythling where at least once I spotted the Cierva Airhorse Autogiro with its three rotors.

From a very early age I used to devour books on aviation. I consumed pictures of aircraft and their names to be recalled years later. One book suggested that autogiros would be the inter-city transport of the future. I do not remember the book which showed the three rotor Cierva. But I was certain of it as soon as I saw it. It could have been the same book from which I learned about the twin-engined Vimy bomber flown across the Atlantic ocean by Alcock and Brown. But 50 or 60 years later when I saw a flying replica, its name immediately leaped to my recollection.

An interesting day came when we went by train from Preston to Lakeside at the foot of Lake Windermere. The four steam boats on the lake were owned by the railways so we could go by boat to Bowness. Sometimes we might go as far as Ambleside. An evening out was when Uncle George, our mother's brother-in-law, took us by car for a preview of Blackpool Illuminations. As District Engineer for the electricity supply, our uncle had oversight of the famous lights. He once gave my father a bicycle – not new but nonetheless welcome.

The extra bike in the family meant that Dad could give his heavy Co-op one to me. He would have realised that riding a bike would not be easy for me. Unlike my brothers and most children, my mashed-up ears precluded me from many common activities. Climbing trees was no problem but riding a bike was not easily learned. But Dad gave it time. His patience in walking alongside me day after day was wonderful. It seemed out of character from his normal self but he persevered until he was happy to let me go on my own. It was perhaps his greatest gift to me. Time and patience.

Once he was satisfied I could manage, Dad took me for rides. Out to Blackmore and Doddinghurst for a start. Checking the map later, I reckoned we had covered 16 miles that first time. The brow by Fryerning church – known locally as church hill – was a thrill to go down and a severe test to pedal up. Going out in later weeks to see my aunts Highwood way, I found the descent beyond The Viper at Mill Green quite frightening. The sharp decline on a bend was always known as Reeves' Hill, being alongside the cottage of the Reeves family. Another test both for bikes and riders was Beggar Hill. This is straighter but longer and some people have snapped their cycle chains attempting to pedal up the slope.

After a few afternoons exploring the lanes and testing the gradients, Dad and I began making social calls. He no doubt would previously have been visiting his relatives alone but now, with me as a riding companion, he seemed to quite enjoy the visits. For the first he took me to see his Uncle Tom and Aunt Polly. They lived just into the Highwood Quarter at the bottom of Cock Lane. In earlier times there had been a Cock Inn somewhere near. Uncle Tom had been a platelayer on the railway but in retirement he rarely stirred from his chair. He was quite deaf but seemed content to sit in silence.

With experience, I began making visits alone. Learning that I was interested in birds, Aunt Polly told me that Uncle Tom would feed the birds each morning in their back garden. Standing calmly and silently with his arms outstretched, various songbirds would perch on his arms, hands and cap to feed. But I could never be there early enough to witness the sight. Aunt Polly was another fascinating person. Her godly character was easily offended by what she considered to be coarse language heard on the radio. I was more taken by her fingers being double-jointed.

It would have been about that time that I was persuaded to join the Boy Scouts. I went with my brother Peter to the leader's cottage on the edge of

Mill Green common. The Scouts and Cubs were under the direction and leadership of a Miss Christie whom all seemed to agree was unsuitable for the task. In her youth she may have been ideal. Experiences with her brother when they had a large semaphore machine sounded interesting. But in our time there, while she was nursing her invalid mother, she was not giving the lead we needed. One distinct benefit I gained was in learning map reading. Besides compass alignment, I was fascinated to examine a six-inch-to-the-mile map of the local area which depicted such items as garden ponds.

Long before I was able to ride a bike, Dad took me on foot one day to visit his Uncle Tom and Aunt Polly. This may have been a time when my brothers were in school and I was convalescing after some weeks in hospital. Snow lay deep on the ground and we reached the bottom of Cock Lane by a footpath through the woods. Walking through the snow was good exercise for me. Dad had a few words with Uncle Tom who went to work in his shed while we set off for another snowy walk. Although born a Cockney, my father attended school at Highwood and grew up to be familiar with this rural area of Essex.

My father remembered a green lane connecting Cock Lane to the road at Loves Green. The weather being as it was, even green lanes were white that day, along with everything else. We had a good visit with my father's sister Elsie in one of the Loves Green council houses before making our return. The beauty of that cross country walk thrilled me. Where the snow swept off the fields by overnight winds was pushed through and under hedges, it took on shapes to rival any iced cake. Even tinges of colour had been acquired. I remember some pink surfaces in places.

Back at the Cock Lane cottages, Uncle Tom in his shed had constructed a sledge for me to drag home. Those oddments of fence timbers with a length of sash cord were treasured for years. My brothers and I spent many happy hours giving each other rides in snow or on frozen ground. Uncle Tom and Aunt Polly had a son named Tom. He was Transport Officer at Crompton Parkinson. My step-sisters, Ivy and Kath knew him as "Transport Uncle Tom". He once took a sixpence from his waistcoat pocket for me. There was also "Brentwood Uncle Tom" who lived and worked on the big Thorndon Park estate before the mansion was destroyed by fire.

Much is said and written about the Chelsea Flower Show, the world's greatest Spring Flower Show. But I count it a privilege to have been to the world's greatest Summer Flower Show at Southport. The year was probably 1950 or perhaps 1949 when the show was large and magnificent. It made a big impression on me before I left school and became a gardener. Although I enjoyed my small garden at home and did well with my garden at school, I had no thought of gardening full time. My father hoped to have me employed on the railway where he had spent much of his life. I believe it was at Bedfont station that he was a porter in his younger days.

Both my father's brothers were carpenters in their different ways, taking after their father, my Dad's adoptive father. Uncle Tom being Estate Carpenter for wealthy employers and Uncle Joe succeeded his father as builder, carpenter, joiner and undertaker. So my father would hope I might be taken on by the railway as a woodworker. The plan was for me to obtain a job at the Temple Mills carriage works at Stratford. My efforts at school in woodwork were never good but in metalwook my pieces were often commended and sometimes requested for display in the showcase.

One woodwork teacher asked whether I had been a cowboy and to my reply in the negative, said "Then why the wide open spaces?" (in the joints.) Whereas in metalwork I enjoyed and eagerly went at the set tasks with praiseworthy results. I was as handy with a file as with a soldering iron. Sadly, I was again in hospital when brazing and forging were taught. We should perhaps have expected that I might have some difficulty obtaining full time employment. My parents may have discussed that possibility but I caught a train to London, met my father at Liverpool Street station and went with him to see the Medical Officer at Marylebone station.

The Railway doctor soon found reason to reject me. Being rejected for railway employment was a great disappointment for me and perhaps greater for Dad. But he asked only if I was found colour blind, as he knew an experienced Signalman who lost his job after being found colour-blind. But it was my ears, not my eyes, that were the problem. This was the first of a succession of failed medical examinations. A blow to my pride, if not to my dignity. All my life thus far had been aimed at proving myself to be as good or better than my brothers. What next?

With the Easter 1951 holidays, I left school along with my classmates but had no job to go to. My mother was not pleased to have me aimlessly idling around home. I needed help but knew not where that might be found. My brother David had a job on Willie Steven's farm, Master John's mixed farm beyond Mountnessing. David enjoyed working with the dairy herd. Besides the cows to be milked twice each day he had plenty of variety. He was needed there but no one seemed to need me. Help came from the milkman who told Mum that a Mr Brand in Pemberton Avenue wanted a boy.

Dick Brand was Gardener / Chauffeur / Factotum for Mr John Miles and his family. They lived in Fryerning on the road to Blackmore. The big house, with its walls half hung with clay tiles, was called The Tiles in Victorian times. When Mr Miles bought the house it was renamed Barn Mead. Dad and I cycled out there to see Mr Miles who was interested to hear a little of the history of his home. My father's adoptive father used to contract with wealthy people to work on their estates. He would contract for painting and decorating, using paints mixed by hand from the raw materials. Also constructing and hanging gates and similar estate maintenance. I heard from Dad that in his youth he had to help mix paints. He also told me of watching his 'father' light a fire to char the bottom end of gateposts to preserve them in the ground.

Mr Miles would have heard that my father spent much of his spare time in jobbing gardening at several places around Fryerning. The Bays and Spilfeathers were two where I had helped him. They agreed for me to start on a weekly wage of two Pounds. This seemed to me too little when boys I had been at school with had motorbikes. I had my dad's old Co-op bike which served to get me the one-and-a-quarter miles for work at 8 a.m. At first I was cycling with Dick Brand each way. We rode home for lunch at 1 p.m. and back for 2 p.m. till 5 o'clock finish. Besides 8 till 12 Noon on Saturdays.

Being a good reader helped me to learn and I have collected Gardening Books down the years. Dick Brand was very good at preparing vegetables for the showbench but he was unskilled in other areas. He would know most names of things he had planted, trees, bulbs and so on. But not plant names in a general sense. He taught me several types of digging and trenching. Pricking out seedlings, watering from below, hedging and haymaking etc. My first pay rise came when "The Guv'nor" heard that I was using the motor lawnmower.

My weekly Forty shillings became Forty-five and the Pound I had to give my mother was also expected to increase. An incidental benefit was that – like David on the farm – I qualified for the extra ration of cheese.

It seemed hard saving for a better bicycle when boys I'd been at school with were riding motorbikes. One of the jobs I learnt at Barn Mead was to spray the fruit trees. I took a keen interest in this because one lesson I remembered from my limited schooling was on syphons, pumps and syringes, using glass tubes. Syphoning could be done by simply using a length of hose but the hand pumps and syringes we used were of brass. I perfectly understood the action of our double-acting brass spray pump with its rubber hose and interchangeable nozzles because the glass bodied ones at school had so interested me.

Having chronic hearing difficulties seemed to make me more determined than usual to have radio as a hobby. Two tins with a piece of string was fun at first but before long I wanted electronics. My younger brother John and Bill Hart next door were collecting secondhand parts of real radios. I helped them build crystal sets and parts were sometimes given to me. One set I built consisted of little more than a large switchable coil. But no matter the setting it was switched to, that receiver never picked up anything but the BBC Home Service. One programme they broadcast was called Twenty Questions or Animal, Vegetable or Mineral. A fourth denomination used less frequently was Abstract. This may have been chosen when I heard the sepulchral voice of Norman Hackforth intoning "A flying saucer, a flying saucer."

Our family radio was in use every evening. Its large cabinet of veneered plywood stood on an oak chest of drawers beside Dad's armchair. When my father was away on shift work or in bed, this was my chosen seat. With one ear almost clamped to the loudspeaker I could follow the programmes well enough. In hospital for further surgery during my teen years, I learnt something of Short Wave propagation. My next piece of kit was a Johnson's Globe King one valve Short Wave receiver. I spent too much trouble trying to build a case to house it when most users might have been satisfied without one. This was about the time Johnson's Radio were moving from Macclesfield to Worcester. Or the other way perhaps? My memory is hazy of those days in my first job. I tried using off-cuts from Mrs Miles' new kitchen for housing my Globe King.

My increases in pay never exceeded five shillings and from the start I had to give Dick Brand my portion of the National Insurance stamp. So in April 1951 the £2 cash from The Guv'nor's hand became a single Pound as soon as I reached home. Less anything I parted with over the week-end and minus the National Insurance payment on Monday morning. I felt forced to beg for increases. Mr Miles always listened carefully and wanted to know my plans almost to the last penny. He would have believed it good training for me. I never knew if he treated his own children in like manner. Most humiliating for me was his practice of always promising more if and when I did extra to earn it. A carrot for the donkey?

After one of those five shilling increases and I was prepared to cycle home, Dick Brand asked me if anything was said regarding Sunday working. No, nothing. But from then on, it was my job to go in on alternate Sundays to collect the eggs, feed the poultry, check on the ponies, fill coal scuttles, the log basket and replenish the kindling wood. Plus in winter shovelling out the boiler ashes and stoking the boiler besides replenishing the coke supply for later. We did as much as possible on Saturday mornings so as to avoid jobs such as shoe polishing on Sundays.

During that time in the early 1950s I used to cycle on Sunday afternoons to watch the jet fighters at North Weald Aerodrome. They were flown by pilots of the Royal Auxiliary Air Force. Each with a Meteor F8. A beautiful single-seat aircraft. One of them sometimes towed a canvas target for the others to attack over the North Sea with their guns. A young airman would hold back the target until the Meteor had just begun to move. The drag of the target caused the plane to fly with a strange nose-up attitude. One afternoon I saw a Canberra bomber far away across the airfield. Later the RAF Fighter Command flew Hawker Hunter fighters from there. I have watched a formation take-off by four Meteors together making less noise that a single Hunter.

While working at Barn Mead I frequently had chances to watch aircraft. And the geese with one eye cocked to the heavens would inform me of a high-flying plane unheard overhead. Two massive B36 bombers at a great height were once spotted because of the geese. And each year I could watch aircraft of the various RAF Commands rehearsing for the Queen's Birthday Flypast. Most memorable of these was when Coastal Command took their turn. Eighteen Avro Shackletons in formation were used for the Flypast but I could admire twenty-one of them rehearsing daily. It was a joy when III squadron of Fighter Command became the official aerobatic team. Forerunners of the famous Red Arrows, they flew from North Weald and were a great pleasure. Time after time I could see them practicing their varied programme around and over me.

The year I began work was one year after I had joined the Boys Own Club. Ingatestone Boys Own was started in 1919 as a Sunday Bible Class for a few choir boys of Ingatestone parish church. Miss E. Vera Pemberton, daughter of the Rector, conducted the Bible Classes and pretty well everything else. The club expanded as boys from quite a wide area cycled over for the various activities on different evenings. The reason my brother Peter and I were encouraged to join was that, although tall we were not robust and Boys Own had a keen PT night on Thursdays. The rule that all members should attend the Sunday Bible Class was bent for Pete and me because of our Elim connection.

Club nights were held in the Parish Rooms in Stock Lane. We soon were regularly attending the popular Monday Games Nights besides Thursday PT classes. It was on Mondays at Boys Own that I began to know other boys besides those I knew at school. Older and younger than my own year group. Being placed for a year or two in a school class with younger boys helped to an extent but at Boys Own we formed a wider range. Some boys had a need to be active and the billiard table was always fully booked. Others of us were happy to sit reading. There were copies of Punch and the National Geographic magazines which I enjoyed.

I became one of a clique with David Sorrel (always known as Jimpy) and Bob Warren, Gordon Lincoln and maybe one or two others less memorable. Jimpy was the leader of the Nature Club which met weekly in the Club Leader's attic. One time, the club received a visit by the Duke of Gloucester, patron of the National Association of Boys Clubs. The large number of current and former club members wanting to be there meant that most had to congregate outside the Parish Rooms while a select few of us would be inside representing a normal club night. For this, Derek Palmer and I were at a card table pretending to play chess.

Miss Pemberton conducted the Duke around the room, giving HRH a few brief descriptions of various club activities and introducing members. At our table she told him that Philip was leader of the Nature Club and "Derek is very good at running". He was too. We heard that he ran for his regiment in Germany. After the annual Ingatestone Flower Show one time, Jimpy Sorrel offered to take me badger watching. He had permission through Skipper Seymour to enter Mrs Upton's Wood at Mill Green. Although it was high summer when the animals leave their setts during twilight, sounds from the noisy funfair at the Show would have disturbed the badgers and we saw only one that evening.

As we cycled home from my first badger watching, Jimpy had to report to "Skipper" Seymore. He would have obtained our permission to enter Mrs Upton's woods but I never told him when I went alone. Jimpy had us perching on a branch well above ground but I thought it better to stand. Finding a place downwind of the sett, when I went alone I stood to watch. First a mouse was active nearby. Then some midges busied themselves above the sett entrance. This was the signal for the emergence of the first badger. Soon a small group of badgers were rolling around scratching themselves. While the young ones stayed near their home, I watched the old boar hurry away before I left to cycle home.

Mr and Mrs Miles had four children, two boys and two younger girls. Christopher and Martin were mostly away at boarding schools. Sarah was at Preparatory in Chelmsford while little Vanessa was starting pre-school in Fryerning Parish Room. This was always "The Jam Factory" to my father because during the War the W.I. (the Women's Institute) made jam and rose-hip syrup there. Outside The Jam Factory was a horse pond and it was interesting to watch Mr Tydeman drive his pony and trap into it to cool the iron tyres. The pony could also take a drink from the pond.

Years later, I discovered that the garden where I began my working life had formerly been noted for its arboretum. There were a number of unusual old apple trees widely scattered around but these were not much valued. Before the Miles' had moved there, Dick Brand had planted a small orchard of thirty young fruit trees. Much was expected of these but on cold heavy clay they did not thrive. Towards the end of my employment there, I spent much time over five weeks digging drainage channels to improve the soil. This work was very successful as I was informed later.

Some of the other trees were interesting but no one knew or cared much about any of them. Before I worked there a cedar of unknown variety was removed from the lower lawn and one of a pair of London plane trees was taken out during my time. Tom Green's tree men cut it down and removed the major part but the enormous stump proved too difficult for their machinery. So Dick and I had to dig round it and saw the monster into managable pieces using hand saws. Another time Tom Green's men came and felled a big white poplar. A young Davidia involucrata remained.

A few years later when Dick Brand had left, Mr Miles got me to take out a gleditsia triacanthos. This ought not to have been done. It was the rarest tree we had but Mr Miles had assumed it was the same as a big tree on the lawn. This was probably a Pseudoacacia or some type of Robinia. Both trees bore thorns but otherwise they were quite dissimilar. That gleditsia was about six inches in diameter and should have been left to mature. But I had little education or self confidence to speak my mind. In fact my self confidence grew and I was gradually increasing in knowledge.

Still in my first year there, I requested and was allowed a day off to visit London. While working on the farm my brother David had found a balloon bearing a ticket from the Festival of Britain. Two visitors would be given free admission to the South Bank Exhibition through finding the balloon. The trip certainly added to my meagre education. Situated among the exhibits in the great Dome of Discovery I remember the recently invented float glass of Pilkingtons. One whole vertical pane about 30 feet long and perhaps eight feet high. Another exhibit was intended to demonstrate the airflow across an aircraft wing with a few discrete streams of smoke.

I had read of this recent invention and longed to see it in action. There was a control wheel to vary the angle of incidence of the wing section but visitors were barred from touching it. A few minutes after we first saw it, a man came up and with his back to the machine, he put one hand on the wheel. My frustration rose as he began to stir up the smoke by blindly waggling the short wing section. Seeing someone employed with a purpose and doing it busily but incompetently always annoys me. The man was fortunate that I was not his employer.

There was plenty of variety in my work but I felt the lack of serious teaching. I was keen to learn the names of plants and processes but these were not available. There again I felt frustrated. The first novelty of using the Atco 14" mower soon wore off. In fact I found it more interesting when the transfer port became blocked and the machine had to be "decoked". At certain times I had to use the Allen motor scythe which was never pleasureable. The speed was governed by ignition control. Thus making eight-stroking and sixteen-stroking quite normal besides unpleasantly noisy. Only when it was working hard was the sound more bearable.

One lesson I learned from Dick Brand was in rolling. Our old water-ballast roller could be used to give a light or a heavy rolling. Lawns rarely needed rolling but I was taught to go quickly in such cases. The gravel drive required rolling frequently. It was constantly being churned up by vehicle tyres and in wet weather I learned to roll it slowly. The time taken to press down the top stones into the lower gravel during wet weather improved the drive considerably. This was my occupation one day when Dick had left and Colin Pigeon worked at Barn Mead.

One such wet day my slow walk up and down was rewarded when I spotted a rare object in the gravel. From the muddy surface of the drive, I picked up a piece of jewellery. What I later heard was called a dress clip, perhaps about five centimetres across, was quickly slipped into a back pocket to dry out in my jeans. I guessed it would belong to Mrs Miles but she and the Guvnor were away that day and the object appeared too valuable to mention to the Kitchen staff when I went in as usual for tea. The next day I offered it to "The Missus" expecting to be thanked. I was surprised when, with barely a word to me, she almost flew into the house.

I later learned that a Garden Party had been held with a marquee on the field with many guests attending. Colin Pigeon and the house staff had searched for that piece of valuable jewellery but no one had bothered to inform me about it. A lady in a white Jaguar car came later to collect her diamond dress clip and I was led to expect some form of thanks. In fact I never met her and no thanks was forthcoming. My one regret was that I never counted the diamonds. They may well have numbered up to fifty in total.

That old Allen scythe was one of the early models with declutching performed by a swift jerk down on the handlebars. My next employer had the later model with declutching executed by merely flicking a small catch. They were quite powerful machines and at times the mower fingers would become stuck into a tree, fence or a gatepost. Thus making the required downward jerk to declutch impossible. Using the heavy Arun sawbench was far riskier but more interesting. It had a single cylinder JAP motor which blew splendid smoke rings. There was also the livestock to add interest.

To keep me busy there were laying hens and pullets, a few ducks and geese and sometimes turkeys. For a time we also had a few bantams and some Old English Game fowl. There was also Sarah's pony that was named Mischief. He made a nuisance of himself by escaping from time to time. When my brother Peter came home from delivering newspapers round Beggar Hill, he several times said "Your pony's out again". His way of escape was a mystery until one day when I saw him in the act. He merely ducked his head and put one front hoof between the top and lower strands of barbed wire. It was then a simple matter of putting his head through followed by his remaining three legs and plump body. He was then free to either stroll or gallop off.

We were allowed one week leave with pay each year and I arranged to go cycling one Summer with my father. We rode to Shenfield station to put our bikes on a train to London. From Liverpool Street we set off to ride to Waterloo station. Dad's familiarity with so many different areas of London appeared magical. He had probably walked between Liverpool Street and Waterloo plenty of times but he was inexperienced with modern traffic signals. He assumed the green filter arrows meant that we should turn that way. I heard him call out "I don't know this way" as we pedalled on. However, we were in plenty of time at Waterloo to load our bikes into the Guard's van. Arriving at Southampton we set off to ride out to Wellow.

My father's eldest daughter, my step-sister Dorothy, a fine Christian of the Roman Catholic persuasion, had a bungalow at East Wellow but she was then working at The Vine, Ower. Before we rode there Dad took me out to Nursling and Nursley to look up some acquaintances of his younger days. We quite easily met up with a woman who remembered my father from years earlier. She must have been a relative of Dorothy's mother who was a Hampshire girl. Her name may have been Ivy. While Dad and this woman reminisced, her teenage daughter stood nearby and I decided to break the ice as it were. Being inexperienced with girls, it seemed to me right to take a step in her direction and say something like "Hullo, what do they call you".

To my utter chagrin, before I had made my first move, Dad called out "He's shy". Why can't a twice married man of the world allow a youngster to live his own life? From a feeling of opening up to gain experience, I felt forced backward. Did the old man think he was helping one of us? Being deaf certainly did not make it easy for me to approach strangers but a successful first attempt might have had lasting benefit. I shall never know. Other girls closer to home with prior knowledge of me would surely be more difficult to befriend. My enforced failure hung over me to forestall any future attempt.

On one day of that week, we took a train from Southampton to Weymouth. Outside Weymouth we visited some distant relatives or friends of my father. I believe the woman's name was Beatie and her husband was another Fred. There was a large fuschia riccartonii growing up the wall beside the door. The largest I'd ever seen. The woman came to the door at my father's knock and immediately called out, "Fred!" And a rapid: "Come-and-look-at-this-tall-boy." I would then be seventeen years old and embarrassed. The only other thing I remember of that visit was when my Dad and the other Fred were left to talk and Beatie took me away to lean from the window. The cottage was built over a river and Beatie fed a trout which lived underneath in secret.

The rest of our cycling week passed easily enough. It was interesting to see the watercress growing around Kings Somborne and a few memorable country pubs. One day we stopped for a drink at the thatched Sir John Barleycorn at Cadnam and further on alighted to read the inscription on the iron-clad Rufus stone. Some memories from that week are confused in my mind with those from subsequent years cycling with my brother Peter and motor-cycling alone. Pete and I planned to cycle all the way. Riding from Ingatestone to Romsey and Wellow, the wind was against us all day and my bike, a Phillips Jaguar, was new and stiff in its bearings. Pete's bike was well run in and so was mine – for the homeward journey.

Pete and I had a good week. Staying with our sister Dorothy and going for days out on our bikes. The day I best remember was when we decided to leave our bikes and take the Ferry to the Isle-of-Wight. Our parents had taken us by ferry to Ryde but we were too late for that and spent the day in Cowes. Shops we walked past were yacht-chandlers and similar suppliers of boating equipment. This made a pleasant change for us Essex boys. Best for me was discovering the Saunders-Roe Princess flying boat. Three were built and this one had the top of its tail fin removed to fit into the hangar. The remaining two I remember were berthed at Calshot.

After I became the new owner of an old 98cc two-stroke James Comet motor-cycle, it seemed right to trust it to take me for a holiday in Hampshire and Wiltshire. The weather was fine until Gates Corner on Eastern Avenue. The rain that began there was still falling as I rode through Staines. All round the North Circular, I was glad of my rubber coat and a pair of Dad's leggings from the railway. But my shoes were full of water and my socks were soaked. I stopped at a boot and shoe shop in Staines and asked whether they had some sub-standard or inexpensive wellingtons.

I was pleased to find they had just such boots but the salesman recommended buying a better, heavy-duty pair. I told him I had a good pair for work and wanted only a cheap pair for riding. That old James Comet had leg shields and panniers on frames and I went outside to take a clean, dry pair of socks from one pannier. Back in the shop I sat wringing the water from the wet socks onto the carpet. I felt much happier with new dry socks and boots to ride in. The friendly salesman suggested I throw the bike over the wall and continue my journey by train.

Ignoring his advice, I continued on my holiday. Only to find at my destination that rain had been splashing upwards during much of my journey to penetrate the pannier bags and into their contents. My pyjamas were hung above Dorothy's open fire before I could wear them. Riding on my own that week, I was able to explore places previously beyond reach. I witnessed a mock emergency at Hurn airport and watched a Skeeter helicopter being speedily hopped back and forth over a hangar at Eastleigh. First called Swaythling, then Eastleigh and in its most recent incarnation Southampton International. Just as Hurn became Bournemouth International.

More important and more memorable than any of our holidays was an occurrence in the year of my seventeenth birthday. After we moved out from East Ham, my parents had begun attending the Elim church in Ingatestone. And we boys were in the 3 pm Sunday School each week beside being with our parents in the morning and evening meetings. A telephone engineer named Lloyd from Post Office Telephones was the Ingatestone Elim Pastor. Even as a small child, I felt a love for Mr Lloyd. He (or perhaps his father) may have been adopted as a child mascot by Welsh troops serving in the Peninsular War. There was certainly a Spanish look about his eyes.

After a year or two, Mr Lloyd was replaced as Pastor by a Miss Gladys Garton. She was a Canadian and a former Salvation Army officer. When I was seventeen, Miss Garton enthusiastically informed my parents of Divine Healing meetings being conducted in Southend. She thought it a good opportunity for my ear troubles to be prayed over. I felt encouraged to take half a day off work and went with my parents to the church in Southend where an Evangelist named Ludovic Barrie was holding meetings. That afternoon gathering was probably on a Thursday and therefore most of the people were mature women.

Mr Barrie wanted all those desiring personal prayer to sit in the front row of chairs. Being a tall slender youth, I would have looked quite out of place in that gathering. But I had been listening to the Evangelist's talk and was concentrating on that. There was no long reading from the Bible. And no long dry talk. He gave us just the first two verses of Chapter six in the Epistle to the Hebrews. Hebrews 6: 1 & 2 came to stir me to a fresh way of seeing the Christian life. I had been in church every Sunday for most of my life. Apart from weeks in hospital or otherwise unwell, Sundays meant being at church morning, afternoon and evening

I had read much from the Bible and remembered much Christian teaching. In many ways I must have been a typical teenager believing there would be little new for me to learn in later years. But these two verses hit me with some force. I well knew that new aircraft were being developed every year and we could all see new vehicles coming onto the roads. But new things in the Christian life!? Tell me more – can this really be happening to me? What was stirring in me was a new dose of faith. I knew the bible teaches that to please God, faith is required. But is there more to learn? I wondered.

The Evangelist went along the row, praying for each person in turn. I do not remember whether he wanted the ladies to stand but he certainly ask me to stand up. He was rather portly and stood less than medium height as he reached up to put his fingertips into my ears. His prayer made no impression on me and most likely was not remembered by anyone present. But God heard. The Holy Spirit took his words and acted there and then. My ears, which had been dug out a few times and "mashed up" as someone once said, were pretty useless for hearing. I had no eardrums and the tiny bones of hearing – three in each ear – were long gone.

But suddenly I could hear clearly. Mr Barrie wanted to test my powers of hearing. Taking hold of his watch chain, he began hauling his timepiece over the horizon. In a flash, I remembered my own watch and held it to my ear. Never being able to hear it previously, I could now listen to its steady tick. The little man left me where I stood and went to the back of the hall. He carried out a brief conversation with me and then made an announcement. "There are healings," he said, "And there are miracles. "That was a miracle!"

That must have been the year my brother David became a soldier. National Service meant that most boys would go into one of the Armed Forces. Some were glad to go but always a few were unwilling. My youngest brother, John, went into the Royal Navy straight from school at fifteen years of age. David was more reluctant but he was persuaded to join the RAMC. When based at Millbank Hospital, he helped to man the First Aid post at Earls Court for the Royal Tournament. He was 3½ or 4 inches over my 6 feet in height and he took quite a liking to the little Gurkha soldiers. Sailors would go to the First Aid post for sticking plaster to protect their hands when on the ropes and window ladders.

It was the rule that you would have a chest x-ray some months before having to join the Forces at age eighteen. I was therefore only seventeen when I took the chance to volunteer for army life when I had to attend for the x-ray. The colour sergeant had gone into town for his lunch so my interview was with the C.O. a Major Cox. He soon guessed that I had some difficulty in hearing and told me I would be unlikely to pass medical inspection. I ought to have realised this but was so keen to serve in the Armed Forces that I could consider little else.

Seeing my disappointment, Major Cox gave me some little encouragement. He told me to wait until I was called for the Medical and then if I passed that, to volunteer again. After the 'PULHEEMS' and I was refused, I ardently enquired a reason for refusing me my ambition. The M.O. (doctor) at the end of the line could say no other than that my health could break down at any time. To be charitable, I must admit that over the ensuing 55—60 years, I have not remained fully fit. But I was then young, keen and bitterly disappointed.

Even so, in my youthful yearning I refused to accept the facts. Taking a coupon I cut from a newspaper, I enquired for information regarding the RAF. They sent me a Rail warrant to attend for their Medical and et cetera. With yet another day off work, I found my way to the RAF offices at Redbridge where I was welcomed and treated kindly, but still refused. "Isn't there something I can join" I protested, and asked about the ROC. My father's brother Tom had served many years in the Royal Observer Corps and this seemed to be my answer. If not my salvation.

After Southend for the Army and Redbridge for the RAF, to attend interview for the ROC, I had to go no further than Billericay. Two training meetings were held monthly and I was interviewed at one of these. And with that I became a member of the Royal Observer Corps. No stress. Apart that is from arriving late for interview. I did not know Billericay then and the bus took me further than I intended. I used the bus because I wanted to look respectable. Thus began my contribution to the Cold War of the 1950s. For the training meetings I biked over. Six-and-a-quarter miles each way meant that my mileage allowance was worth having.

I had a lot to learn. We all had to be familiar with the phonetic alphabet and I quickly memorised Able Baker Charlie Dog Easy Fox et cetera. I had completed learning this ready to use, when that alphabet was replaced by the International version. So I then had to learn Alpha Bravo and so on. I think we were all pleased when Charlie and Mike were resurrected from the previous version. Most of the training could be done at home as we were provided with pictures and drawings of many British and foreign aircraft types. A section of the Official Secrets Act had to be signed. The Beaufort Scale for weather reports was also included in our training.

Before becoming an Observer in uniform, I already knew many of the aircraft of various nations. With the help of professional training materials, I became quite adept at recognising and naming aircraft of most European and American types. My Uncle George from Preston once asked me if I could use that ability for Bible knowledge. I remember we were out walking at the time. We were passing the Mill Green water tower when I was struck by his suggestion. Such a thought had never occurred to me before but I believe it has helped as I have continued to read the Bible. Familiarity with God's word has become a pleasure – but more of that later.

Just before joining the ROC, I spent a very special holiday camping in the Lake District. Uncle George invited me to join him, my Aunt and James, their youngest son, under canvas. My uncle was very familiar with the whole area and drove up from Preston to pitch camp on a farm at Ellers Brow, near Elterwater. They met me at Ambleside after I travelled north by coach and bus. During that week we drove by car to most of the lakes and to others by local buses. One day we went up Great Langdale to Dungeon Ghyll and walked up to Stickle Tarn.

Uncle George knew this route well from having worked there. He told me that two men used to walk up each morning to release water from the tarn to drive the machinery at the mill. Westmoreland green slate was sawn by water power into blocks and slabs. As an Electrical Engineer, Uncle George had once converted the mill to run on mains electricity. Arriving at Stickle Tarn, we picnicked by the water before going over Pavey Ark and down to Grasmere on the further side. People train on Pavey Ark in rock-climbing but we went up the easy way. Two girls lay on the top on the dry grass.

The stretch from the top down to Grasmere I was told, is often boggy underfoot, but it was very dry the week of our holiday. I retain a unique memory of that walk. We met maybe four or five shepherds taking their flocks down to farms in the valley and I was thrilled to see each man running four dogs. From Grasmere we returned to our camp by bus. Another exceptional memory from that week is of seeing Donald Campbell's speedboat "Bluebird" in the boathouse at Ullswater. I never knew if a charge was made for our visit there. It was in total an inexpensive holiday for me.

I am always pleased to see a picture of the Langdale Pikes. We began our walk one day on the far side and walked over Harrison Stickle and Pike of Stickle and on down to Dungeon Ghyll. During our week we happened to meet Horace and Elsie Butler who were on furlough from the Belgian Congo. One day our small camping party went with Horace and Elsie to the coast at Silecroft. I sat on the beach with Horace while the others went in for a dip. I picked up a black and white stone I spotted at my feet and Horace said "That's unique". After all these years, I still have that unique stone.

Having witnessed my fitness in fell walking, Uncle George asked me whether I felt able to do more. He had in mind to take me up Scafell Pike and I acquiesced to this. But it was not to be. During our week's camping, my cousin Muriel was having a day off her nursing in Preston. We went to meet her in Ambleside which took us a day away from other activities. Muriel would have gained more from that day than I lost and this could seem to be my contribution to her career. She became a Mission Midwife in Central Africa.

My uncle and aunt knew the folks at the church in Elterwater and we went there for a splendid evening. Horace Butler had previously trained as an opera singer and in that little Mission Hall he gave us a superb musical recital. First at the piano, he played and sung a hymn given under the Holy Spirit recently to the Congolese Christians. Then he sang in English."My heart is thrilled when'ere I think of Jesus, That precious name that sets the captive free, The only name in which I find salvation..." Horace Butler was tall and the ceiling was fairly low. His powerful singing voice might well have raised the roof.

Back at my work, I reminded 'the Guvnor' that he had promised to teach me to drive when I was old enough. He didn't have time, of course, but he asked the AA and they recommended a driving school in Chelmsford. I went by bus for weekly lessons and ought to have desisted after the first one. The instructor taught me practically nothing and seemed almost asleep a good deal of the time I was paying for. During my sixth lesson, he really frightened me. After that I had to change. Mr Miles then arranged for me to learn with a Mr Deasley of Shenfield. He was excellent and taught me well. Only we used engine braking with the clutch rather than using the brakes as is done now.

When I had passed the driving test, Mr Deasley took me back to where I had left my James motorbike. Referring to my 'L' plates he said he hoped I could soon remove them. The day I was leaving work to take the motorcycle test, a large bough fell from an old elm tree in front of me. The iron gate was severely damaged in the fall and the shock I felt quite put me off from continuing to the Test Centre. One thing and another made my eventual passing the motorcycle test occur exactly 12 months to the day of my parting from Mr Deasley.

It was expected that I would add driving to my gardening, poultry-keeping and other duties. I sometimes drove Mrs Miles' small Ford but the important job was in driving the Humber Supersnipe to London Airport either with the Guv'nor alone or sometimes with all the family. That Humber replaced the Rolls Royce Phantom III which I helped to wax polish before I could drive. Heathrow was the only London Airport then with its three runways and two terminals. When they were overseas I might have to spend nightime hours waiting for a return flight. And this with no extra pay. What I received for Monday to Friday and four hours each Saturday had to cover for Sundays and late nights too.

My little James, with or without 'L' plates, was handy for attending the twice-monthly ROC Meetings and for my daily journeys between Fryerning and Brentwood. I remember telling it, "Home, James, and don't scare the horses". In the meantime, the pre-war plans for building a by-pass of Ingatestone were revived and our row of New Cottages would be demolished. Consequently my mother bought a cottage in Brentwood. This brought far-reaching changes to us all. My youngest brother, John would marry Anne, eldest daughter of Pastor Harold Young. After leaving the Tank Corps and resuming civilian life, brother Peter married his first wife Sheila, daughter of Len 'Smoky' Homewood. Also for me, the prospect of that six-and-a-half miles between Brentwood and.Fryerning in all types of weather made me decide to buy my first car.

After the Elim in Ingatestone we began attending the AoG Church in Brentwood where there were a number of young people who met together on Sunday evenings. Mr and Mrs Tom Felton had two nubile daughters in this group and he encouraged me to join them. My feelings were that he pestered rather than encouraged me but joining them certainly helped me to grow. My greatly improved hearing after the miracle at Southend surely made mixing with strangers far easier. And so it was that I became easier in speaking to girls. They might say I was quite bold.

About this time it became expedient for me to leave my job at Barn Mead and seek other employment. A cottage modernised with a Council grant had to be occupied by a family. So I had to leave and after the clay soil of Fryerning, I was working on very stony ground at Warley where, besides the gardens I had sixteen-and-a-half acres of mostly birch woodland to work in. The car I owned was a pre-war Ford Prefect. First registered in 1944 it had been well used but repaired and resprayed to disguise the rust. I was able to attend for job Interview in my car and this seemed to make a good impression. Working for John Miles had seen my weekly wage rise by 5/- increments from £2 to £7/15/- whereas Lesley Cater had the job advertised at £9 per week.

The Miles and Cater families knew each other and Mr Cater was aware that my weekly wage was no more than Seven pounds fifteen. So he said he would pay me £8 10/- weekly and I replied that I would accept that to start with. Remembering that his offer at the Labour Exchange was £9. My patience was rewarded when, at the beginning of my third week, Mr Cater came to me in the garden before going off to his business. He said, "I'm making your pay Nine pounds from this week, Kelly". "You're earning it." And feeling appreciated, I was encouraged to do even more. Much of the garden and extensive grounds at "Foxburrows" had been neglected. Pruning a neglected row of alternate climbing and rambler roses made a noticeable difference.

Instead of the poultry and ponies I had been used to, I now had pigs to keep. And after the geese at Barn Mead, the Caters had a yellow Labrador who warned me of approaching aircraft. He would track them from one boundary to the other of that fair-sized garden, looking upwards and barking the whole time. The pigs were kept in loose boxes – former stables – with cement floors. We fed them rations of meal carefully weighed out by the staff at Cater Bros in London. Litters of weaner piglets were bought in and raised to bacon weight before they ended on the bacon counters in Cater's stores and supermarkets. Being keen to work hard and prove myself to my own satisfaction, I found it difficult to believe this was unusual. Only years later could I accept that Dick Brand was considered to be lazy.

But Mr Cater's previous gardener was as lazy as could be. The house staff told me he used to spend time grooming the pigs. Kept indoors on clean floors the animals certainly had no need of such attention. I learnt more about this lazy person when the time came for lawn mowing. Unlike the lightweight Atco mowers in my first job – a 14" cut and later a 20"– I now had to manage a very heavy Ransomes machine. I never troubled to measure the size of it but it was extremely weighty with heavy-duty blades. It started with a crank handle and had to be driven from the shed. The shed floor being a few inches lower than the garden path, a strong wooden ramp was required for exiting.

The first time I drove the mower out to begin cutting the newlygrown grass, I was surprised to find the cook come out from her duties to offer her help. She had left her work fully expecting me to need her assistance. That mower needed some muscle to alter its direction and I was appalled to hear that the former gardener had waited on one side of the lawn for this woman to redirect the machine towards him. This was no billiard table surface and the mower could have its direction changed by irregularities. Or so I assumed. Yet this unguided trundling between gardener and cook had been the former practice. I would never let it go beyond my reach and Cook could return to her own work.

On one lawn was a sizeable swimming pool which I had to treat daily in summertime with a measure of chlorine. One side of the pool was sheltered by mature rhododendrons, some of which I cut back to partially uncover the large waterworn limestone rocks beneath. My new employer expressed his appreciation of my work and I told him I planned to have foxgloves and oenotheras planted down the long ride which dropped from the pool area into the wood. Certain aspects of the job I found both encouraging and a challenge. But I surely missed the almost weekly conversations I had become used to with John Miles.

I had grown mentally through the talks I had with Mr Miles and he seemed also to value them. He broadened my education when he showed me around the City of London. My parents had raised us to attend church and Sunday School but it was John Miles who took me to St Paul's Cathedral. He wanted me to find out the purpose of "the model" on display. I told him it was to be a new chapel area in the Cathedral and he immediately expressed disapproval. "Too Catholic" was his comment. He wanted to also show me

Dick Whittington's church and was quite disappointed when we found it locked.

Lesley Cater seemed almost completely occupied by the idea of developing the family business into supermarkets. Having but little interest in his gardens. The pigs were of course a part of his grocery and provisions business. He used to feed his baconers on Sundays, only leaving them to me through the week. We used to weigh them together to check their progress. Although being extended by the job, I began to feel there was insufficient purpose in my work. Some tidying I did using a double- barrelled MacAllan flame gun. But nothing took the place of those conversations with John Miles. And besides feeling a lack of purpose in my job, my home life was not happy.

By this time, encouraged by Tom Felton, I had begun sharing in the after church young people's group. This sharing in some way helped take the place of my conversations with my first employer. The Felton girls and perhaps some of the others had far more education than I and our evenings together were to my benefit. To begin a personal friendship with the opposite gender was a tall order. Growing up with my three close brothers and no sisters of similar age, besides there being just one girl among all the boys at New Cottages left me at a slight disadvantage.

One of our Sunday evening group seemed to take an interest in my personal circumstances. Learning that I was looking for a change through being dissatisfied in my work, Barbara Merry suggested that I could or should apply for employment with the Plessey company at Vicarage Lane, Ilford. Feeling unwelcome at home added to my dissatisfaction. Very soon I had left Caters and was starting with Plesseys at Eddes House, Eastern Avenue, where Barbara worked. Following eight years in mainly outdoor work, I now had a small workshop on the west side of a busy factory. The afternoon sun that summer used to raise the wall temperature to the high nineties Fahrenheit or more. With little fresh air for me.

That workshop was designated for "potting" and "moulding" and I naturally termed it the potting shed. The factory was making synchro motors under licence from Norden Ketay of Rhode Island, N.Y. These small delicate motors, about one inch diameter and a little more in length were extremely fragile and kept in egg trays. Each one had a rotor with silver slip rings moulded onto the shaft end with melamine. The slip rings came with fly leads attached and an ongoing problem had been that the moulding was done in a heated press and the leads were being forced off. I soon realised the problem. This was that all operations were performed to 'spec'. Nothing was permitted outside "spec" – or specification.

I believe an operator could be dismissed without redress if discovered working other than as per spec. But I had been eight years a gardener, used to using my own initiative and at Plesseys I kept my own counsel. Working alone, I was able to turn out good work, never allowing my initiative to be discovered. Which meant that other operators working to spec still turned out 'rejects'. It was not that I worked in secret. Other people continually came into my 'potting shed' which held two ovens and a spray hood. The potting I did used araldite poured under high vacuum conditions by remote control. This caused other problems.

Barbara was working for Plesseys at Eddes House in Chadwell Heath and she was obviously much appreciated. She was a viewing Inspector in Goods Inward and the A.I.B. Inspector offered her a job in his special department. With greater self confidence, she would have done well to accept his offer. But she had even less self confidence than I had. I was a quick learner and could quickly absorb knowledge from books. I was still a gardener when Barbara was expected to use vernier gauges. I had never heard of such things but we went together to the reference library and I was able to explain their use to my girlfriend. From then on she could and did use them in her daily work.

When I began working at Plesseys, I took a packed lunch and usually bought a cheese roll when the trolley came round for mid-morning break. Very different from either of my previous jobs and more like school. I sat just inside the canteen at break time and Barbara sat nearer the front, some distance off. After some weeks Brian, the chargehand, said it was about time I and Barbara began sitting together. He had been a Butlins Redcoat and was a great encourager. Whether we sat together in the canteen I really do not remember but we did walk out together some lunchtimes. I also had some lunchtime walks with an Irish sportsman named Fred Duffy. Fred normally worked in a boot and shoe factory in Ireland but this was closed temporarily.

Their Irish factory manager had been sent to learn modern working methods and Fred had come over to stay with an uncle and aunt in Ilford. Fred Duffy was a marvel. A genuine all round sportsman. Golf, football, fishing, tennis, snooker and a collection of cups for sporting achievements. He studied horse racing and quite regularly made a profit from betting. I had then an Excelsior two-stroke twin motor cycle. One lunchtime Fred asked me to take him to collect his winnings from the Bookmaker's. When he left Plesseys, he intended to spend a month fishing in one lovely area of central Ireland followed by another month fishing in Sligo.

Outside my potting and moulding workshop was a busy machine shop. Nearest to my position were the grinders. Two Fortuna precision cylindrical grinding machines one of which had an attached head for internal grinding. I was encouraged to request an opportunity to train in this highly skilled work. Fred Jones the Foreman loaned me the Fortuna grinder manual to study. Looking back on those days, I am amazed to realise the change this brought to my life. My gardening jobs had required me to operate various lawnmowers, motor scythes, flame guns, a circular sawbench and a chain saw. With no finer measurement needed beyond the length of my boot.

But here I was learning to work to 0·0002" measured by a 0 to 1" micrometer. Outside diameters were required to be finished to within just two tenths of a thousand parts of one inch. As Arnold, my Instructor, said, that was like toolroom standard. Arnold was one of the Dawsons of Leyland and he had previously been grinding crankshaft bearings. Next I progressed to grinding internal diameters which had to be finished to 0·0005" or "half a thou" as we called it. Tiny grinding wheels working out of sight under the flow of cutting fluid. Could anything be further from gardening?

Barbara and I had by then decided to become man and wife, not realising the difficulties we would have in obtaining a home of our own. To become tenants of a Council property, I had to apply to Hornchurch Council for consideration. They invited me to meet someone at their offices in Hornchurch. This was easily done as buses to Hornchurch regularly passed Eddes House. Ariving in Hornchurch I met with someone from the housing department. He explained to me the current situation. This was that no council houses were being built because they had no spare land. Besides this, no one could be added to the waiting list before having been resident in the borough the required number of years.

We would have to be resident so many years and then more years would pass before we could be considered. I could see no reason why I was asked to attend and was not pleased that I had taken time off work. This was of course before the council obtained Hornchurch aerodrome, the "Suttons Farm" site of Battle of Britain fame and now mostly built over. Another consideration was to live in a caravan or mobile home. Enquiring about this drew another blank. I learned that new regulations meant that existing tenants were being evicted from permanent sites. Requirements for hard standings, roads and piped water, meant caravan sites were being restricted in the number of dwellings permitted.

A further consideration was to ask our employer for help with housing. We understood that Plessey had relocated some workers and assisted them with the move and with their re-housing. But this was done only when they required it and such could not be done for us. Barbara's mother suggested that we begin married life with them and this began to look the only answer, although far from what we wanted. We had to realise that life involves hard choices. Our friend Pastor Harold Young advised against a long engagement but thought six months about right.

For better or worse we married in October 1959 and our first home was no more than a bedroom in the small bungalow of Mr and Mrs Merry. They moved into Barbara's small room, letting us have the double bedroom. We had to share the small kitchen and miniature bathroom but it was a start. Mr Merry commuted by bus to his job in Barking and we continued working at Plessey's. Gordon Lincoln had taken the Prefect off my hands when I realised the costs of running it would be too great for me after marriage. We travelled by bus except when I rode the Excelsior twin.

I was doing very well at work with plenty of variety. Sometimes I would be using a big Denbigh press to make melamine pellets for the hot moulding or to stamp out torroidals for stators. But mostly I worked on the Fortuna grinder on internals. Arnold Dawson was usually busy grinding 'o.d.'s while I was trusted to do the 'i.d.'s. In fact a new machine was purchased for grinding internal diameters at very high revs. In America they were using a new material called 'mu metal' and grinding internals at close to 80,000 rpm. Arnold and I agreed that it was not the rpm that mattered so much as the periferal speeds of the small grinding wheels. These were about fingertip size.

The new machine had a high speed oil-mist pneumatic impellor installed alongside to drive the head. And I was its only operator for the time being. But that could not continue for long. By this time Barbara was expecting our first baby and had left work. After I had disposed of the Excelsior motorcycle, I was again travelling by bus. When working overtime, I sometimes rode on the back of the Vespa ridden by Brian, the former Redcoat. After Philip junior was born our lack of privacy became almost too much to bear. Barbara wanted a home and kitchen of our own, away from her mother's interference. I wanted no more than a home to ourselves and a job.

Deciding to move on, I left my native Essex and moved north. Holidays in Lancashire had taught me that vacant houses were plentiful around Preston and Arnold Dawson thought jobs would be available at Leyland Motors where members of his family worked. I therefore decided to up sticks and move north. It was a good job at Plessey's but I had to consider home life. The Bank manager stressed the importance of a secure job but my skilled work was relinquished. I gave in my notice which the Shop Manager was reluctant to accept. Nonetheless I paid a single fare by train to Preston. My mother's sister Phylis in Preston had agreed to take me as a lodger and that seemed all I needed for a limited time.

Barbara had to agree to what would have seemed like a shot in the dark. She wanted to be with me and not with her mother. Not a happy situation but I trusted it would not be for long. Plessey staff even suggested I enquire again for help with accomodation. I emphatically told them I had decided to go and had bought a one way ticket. I had a heavy bag on the handlebars of my pushbike and and it was not easily balanced. Riding along City Road between Liverpool Street and Euston I fell off. A quick look behind told me I was being pursued by a trolleybus and somehow bike, rider and bag hastily reached the safety of the nearside kerb.

Having left Plesseys on the Friday afternoon I was enquiring at Leyland Motors on Monday morning. This was unfortunately not for the best.

They told me they were reorganising and therefore not recruiting just then. But I needed a job and could not wait. "What about this place across the road" I asked. On the opposite side of Golden Hill Lane was BTR and there I tried again for a job. One of the gatekeepers gave me a form to fill in and this I did with no promise of work. I had to understand that Lancashire towns took a week or even two Wakes Weeks when little happened. Mills and Factories closed and holidays were taken *en masse*. Towns such as Leyland, Wigan, Chorley and others would not all take the same weeks but they were annual events.

Preston then had a busy shipping docks and a wide variety of industry and therefore was more like our southern towns. I returned to my lodgings in Preston and in a day or two received a letter requesting me to attend the new BTR rubber works at Farington that Thursday. Most of us in the new intake were required to begin work in the high pressure hose shop. This department worked a four-shift system, never closing for weekends or any public holidays. At first I was with the new group and listened to their instructions such as to beware of the wire.

The rubber hose was threaded through noisy braiding machines wrapping wire of several types round the rubber hose. Steel wire, galvanised, stainless, brass or copper plated. The copper coated wire was particularly to be avoided. A nick from that would be guaranteed to fester, as the Instructor warned the group. But before that first day was out I was transferred to the roller-covering department. I was required to start work on Thursday morning – less than a week since my last job ended. As one of that week's shift, I was also included for Saturday work. The Chargehand, Freddie Madigan, asked if I would mind transferring to nights the following week. More new men were starting and he wanted to avoid us all being on one shift.

I was a new trainee but was pleased to find myself working overtime from the beginning. Saturday mornings when on day shift and alternate weeks working nights at enhanced pay rate. The word 'rubber' is rarely used in the industry. The product is termed 'compound' and is of many types for a multiplicity of uses. We worked at steel tables which could be steam-heated when required. Various types of rolls had to be covered in the specific compound for the type. One of our regular jobs were 'felt rolls' These were covered with vulcanite which is hard and fairly brittle when cured. Felt rolls were twenty or thirty feet long and no more than about 18 or 20 inches in diameter.

A single roll was craned to whichever table it was to be covered at. This was after it had been shotblasted and possibly solutioned. Or we might apply the solution by brush at our table. The compound came in sheets wound onto a spindle between fabric sheeting and we unrolled a suitable length to be trimmed for applying to the roll (or roller). We used two types of knife, both kept sharp. First a short knife used to trim the long edges of the unrolled compound and to cut off the required length. And a longer skiving knife for chamfering edges. Several thicknesses would be needed to build the roller to the required diameter.

After eight weeks apart, Barbara would increasingly want to join me away from her mother and she came up by train with my Preston-born mother. I met them off the train. They had baby Philip, the pram and as much with them as could by piled on top. But our situation was far from ideal. We had a little more space than our single room at Barbara's parents and there we were not left in private. At least Auntie Phyllis did not intrude on us but we had no space for an active toddler to play. After work one day I found almost every surface at the baby's height had been smeared with marmalade by his little hands. One jar spread far.

The bike I brought from Essex sufficed as my transport between Hind St, Preston and my job at Centurion Way, Farington. One winter morning I fell off when returning home from work making the turn off the Penwortham stone bridge onto Broadgate, where the cobble sets were glazed with ice. But far worse happened one morning, riding to work. The main road through Lostock Hall crossed a pair of humped bridges over railway lines. Lancashire weather was often windy and raining at the same time. Like being on a ship at sea. This was the case one particular dark morning as I pushed on against a head wind.

Fortunately there was little traffic but as I pedalled over the two bridges an unladen articulated lorry hit me from behind without warning. If I heard anything it would be the wind and certainly I heard no apporoaching traffic. I flew from the bike in an involuntary swallow-dive and lay face down, stunned, in the nearside gutter with rain-water flowing beneath me. The lorry must have stopped briefly before continuing off the bridge, crushing my bike under its trailer wheels as it passed. The driver helped me up into the lorry's cab, bleeding from a head wound, to await the ambulance. A bus had stopped and its crew took notes but they could offer no help.

In the ensuing ambulance, I was taken to Preston Royal Infirmary in Deepdale Road and then to the Casualty Dept by wheelchair. The right side of my head and face had suffered a heavy blow and two young nurses put two stitches in my torn right eyebrow. They were then ready to discharge me and to continue with the next patient. I told them my knees were both hurt but ignoring my arrival by wheelchair they directed me to walk out. I had never before been hit on the head by a large lorry but the shock persisted. Too dazed to know in which direction to walk, I set off to walk home to Hind Street. A fair distance across town.

Heading mistakenly towards Moor Park, I began to see a little clearer and turned westward. By then it was daylight and one or two people in Fishergate seeing my disfigured face asked what "the other Fellow looked like". That evening I managed to walk round to the Westcliff doctors surgery to show him my inflamed knees. He immediately told me I must not walk another step more. But I offered to clear out of his room as it was not a long walk back to Hind St. He agreed and would send an ambulance next morning. Our accommodation was upstairs and we did not hear when the ambulance came. The next day I sat downstairs in a cold room to be sure and I was taken to see the bone Specialist.

His name was Dr Noblett and I caught a glimpse of something like *Haemostasis* in the notes to explain my severely swollen knees. Like footballs they were and a tight fit in my jeans. I was told to rest and had a month off work. Going by bus I visited the Roller Covering crew and like the men I passed in Preston, Freddie Madigan asked what the other fellow looked like. The right side of my face, bruised and grazed, was first red and blooded, then turned yellow, blue, purple and brown. Besides BTR I also had to see a solicitor. A few weeks later he informed me that the lorry firm was offering £60 in compensation which I refused to consider.

A Preston cycle shop repaired the twisted frame of my bike and fitted a new chain wheel but I insisted on having a new bike as well. My waterproof Gannex cap had disappeared somewhere over the railway and my jacket was torn. I had a month off work besides the pain and inconvenience. So when the young lawyer informed me that he had accepted and signed for £100 on my behalf, I was none too pleased. He said there was nothing I could do but to accept the cheque. I do not remember his fee but am sure he did not lose out.

B ack at Roller Covering, each new length of compound was joined to the previous one on the table. The two cleanly cut edges were damped with a suitable solvent and butted together before being hammered on the table top. We each had a pneumatic hammer and the two lengths of compound could become one before being applied to the roll. We had small hand rollers to apply pressure and a pricker to release trapped air but each building table had a rolling machine to apply pressure along the length of the roll. With the surfaces dampened by a sprinkle of solution and enough pressure, the different layers joined together before being cured. Joins were skived off with a skiving knife. The roll was then craned from the table and the next one brought.

I went to see the works Nurse one day after my fingertips felt something soft protruding from the hole made by Mr Henry behind my left ear. She described it as "something like proud flesh" and arranged for me to be seen by the works doctor on his next visit. He at once said "Oh, it wants curetting". I learnt later that this was his usual brusque manner. A few years later when a toe was injured, he said "Oh, it wants cutting off, it's too long". When he was sent for after a Gatekeeper had collapsed, the doctor passed me in the yard on his way out and said, "You'll have to get a new Gatekeeper, the other one's dead".

T he waiting list for surgery was six months and I had two turns on it. Rather than the operation I expected, that would have possibly removed the polyp, they merely took a slip for biopsy and spent time operating on my right ear which was left very sore. From previous experience I knew that major ops are performed last, after any minor operations. Next day on Ward rounds, the Registrar informed me that the growth in my left ear had first to be checked and opportunity was taken to clean out my right ear. Dead skin and other debris had accumulated through years of neglect. As the Indian Registrar said, "There was lot of muck". No wonder I was sore.

Six months later I was again admitted to the ENT Ward and this time my Op was scheduled last. This went ahead without too much trouble although the anaesthetic used may have been experimental as it seemed particularly powerful. "Like a steam-roller" I said to the Registrar. After time off work and one or two outpatient appointments I was fit to return to work. But the years of neglect were noted. From then on I must return periodically as an outpatient for both my ears to be cleaned out. Ears are designed to be self-cleaning. Jaw movements work to roll particles of wax, dead skin and anything superfluous away to the outside. Repeated surgery left both my ear canals collapsed with accumulated scar tissue partially blocking the opening or *meatus* so they work the opposite way.

By then Barbara and I had obtained a Mortgage and moved into a modern house at Cinnamon Hill, Walton-le-Dale. Modern, but basically two up and two down with a small bathroom. After a time I was able to build a shed but at first my bike, lawn mower and garden equipment were stored in the kitchen. I believe Barbara held this against me far longer than it continued. Buses between Bolton and Lancaster passed nearby although we could not be sure of catching one of those as several other routes passed that way. Because most people would be travelling to Preston they could use any of the buses.

We moved our few belongings from Auntie Phylis's in Hind Street to our new home by wheeling them on and in the pram along the riverside path. Then up the hill from Walton-le-Dale. We were glad to have our own place but we had no luxury. To protect the bare floor boards from the baby's spilled food, we spread newspapers. These papers used to stand upright when the wind came through the floor. We had but one chair at first and entertaining Barbara's parents when they visited us took some thought. A wooden box served as a seat for one and a five gallon drum for another. I sat upstairs on the bed until the first sitting was ended.

I have waited at the nearby bus stop with my head swathed in white bandages to attend the ENT Outpatients Clinic. A surgeon named Mr Wickham once attempted to manipulate my left ear from its collapsed and sunken position and had it standing out like a pea on a drum. A yard or so of narrow gauze was then packed into my ear, bandaged over and I was discharged like a mummy to catch a bus home. On one occasion a Kenyan businessman pulled up and offered us a lift into Preston. I imagined Mr

Wickham pulling at my left ear with both hands with his foot against my jaw or neck. Maybe a week or two later the gauze pack was removed and blood poured from my ear.

Fresh bandages were wrapped around my head and again I was discharged to catch the bus home. Dr Donald, our GP in Bamber Bridge, seemed to panic when he saw the result and prescribed enough cotton wool and gauze pads to last us a few years. Following this my ear collapsed worse than previously. But I survived and returned once again to working life. Dr Donald was a good man as a family doctor. Besides my chronic health problems he once kept me off work for many weeks after I had bronchitis. Our boys once had chicken-pox and when Barbara picked that up, she was extremely ill.

We had a few holidays, outings and visits. Uncle George Atkinson called to see us one Christmas and brought us firewood, vegetables and a frozen duck. It was also by his help that we had obtained a Mortgage at a time when this was difficult. My uncle was surely guided by God and took a fatherly interest in all our circumstances. When I was one of a group around his bed in hospital, it came as something of a shock when uncle George asked me to lead them in prayer. I more often heard him leading in prayer.

My brother David paid for us to hire a car for two weeks. He spent one week with us, letting us have the car a second week to visit family and friends in Essex. Another time Gordon Lincoln visited us and joined us on some coach outings. One trip took in both Ringway (Manchester) Airport and Jodrell Bank which Gordon had seen from the air. He may not have been with us on a day's coach outing we enjoyed around Yorkshire. After visiting Ingleton, Ripon, Harrogate and Blubberhouses Moor, we returned to Preston via Sutton Bank, a popular gliding site.

Being unable or forbidden to join the armed forces like my brothers or even the Railway, Post Office or Police, I was determined to attempt some adventurous pastime before too long. My parents had seemed unwilling for me to ride a motorbike or even a racing pushbike. So I waited till I was Twenty-one (and still unmarried) before going away for a gliding holiday. Comparing severall Gliding Clubs which were advertising holidays with Instruction, I selected the Bristol Club. Formed at Filton, they had vacated that busy place and settled on a long hilltop site near the village of Nympsfield, between Stroud and Dursley.

I had first to go by train to Stroud on a Sunday afternoon. The Ticket Inspector at Paddington with his strong Welsh accent instructed me to change at Swindon. At this junction I had some time to wait and while there I decided to get myself a copy of the ABC timetables book. This was when many trains were steam hauled while some were being converted to Diesel. It was a time of changes and I thought the ABC timetables could make an interesting subject for study in times to come. I was none too pleased to learn some years later that my father had this book thrown out as being out of date. My connection to Stroud, when it arrived, was a small bus followed by a large parcel van. I was the only one of the passengers to permit my small suitcase to be conveyed by the Railway van driver.

At Stroud I had to catch a bus to the Rose and Crown in Nympsfield. We passed by the Gliding Club before reaching the village and with others I was shown to our accomodation in the village pub. Weekends were allocated to Club members while we holiday-makers received instruction from Monday to Friday. It was a good week at the end of June and the weather may have been the best of that summer which was quite rainy in the main. That Bristol Club field was unsuitable for *ab initio* pilots like us but I for one was happy to trust the Instructor to get us safely back onto the field. In the warm weather the thermals were strong and on one flight we reached 1500 feet in a 20-minute flight. I took a black-and-white photograph of Nympsfield village from about 600 feet. Another pilot told me they gained 3000 feet during a half-hour flight.

By the following year, I had bought a car and I booked two weeks at the Bristol Gliding Club. I drove there on a sunny afternoon and enjoyed the journey. Two weeks seemed a good idea after my single happy week the previous year. But the first year had excellent weather for gliding, whereas my second time there enjoyed only one week of good gliding weather. I did not mind too much. I was on holiday and happy to go out to the surrounding area. One man had spent childhood holidays with his grandparents in the Wye valley. He drove us to the Forest of Dean, Monmouth, Chepstow castle and Tintern Abbey. He also remembered the Speech House in the Forest of Dean and took us there. We crossed the Severn first at Over and returned via the former Beachley – Aust ferry.

Another memorable outing that week was to Slimbridge Wildfowl Centre. This was the home of Peter Scott, another member of Bristol Gliding Club. He had bought himself a Slingsby Eagle two seat glider which he named The Sea Eagle. He later presented it to the Bristol Club. He flew off cross country one day, after giving us permission to use his hard-top Land-Rover. I drove it and took the chance to peruse some of his manuscript autobiography which lay on the front seat. The club had a canvas top Land-Rover which we used for cable retrieving. So that week I drove both Land-Rovers.

The intervening weekend between the two weeks for which I had paid had to be kept free for club members. Bill Culpin, a Teacher, suggested going to an Air Display at Colerne on the Saturday. I was happy to take him there and he bought us a meal on the way. That was the best liver I've ever eaten. I remember little from Colerne but one aircraft that I can never forget was a Blackburn Beverley which flew over us with its rear loading doors removed. The sight of that great square open space above us made me wonder: "How does this thing leave the ground like that and stay up there."

For the Sunday I was there, Harold Young had suggested I go to Cam where he had been Pastor in his younger days. I discovered Cam comprises two villages, Upper and Lower Cam. There is but one Free Church between them and I made my way there for the Sunday Morning Service. Afterwards I was invited home to Lunch by a middle-aged mother and her young son. Accepting her invitation seemed the right thing to do but they had no knowledge of Harold Young. The woman's husband appeared to be a semi invalid and he stayed at home for the Morning Service. He entertained us with hymn tunes on the piano by concentrating on the black keys.

I knew the Bible fairly well even in those early days. I had learnt that I should not spread myself around but Jesus had said it was good to stay at one home for the duration. Therefore I was torn between staying at the first home where I enjoyed a bubble-and-squeak meal or going for the evening where they might remember Harold Young. As it happened, they were not keen to befriend a young chap who knew their one time Pastor. So it might have been better to remain where I was first welcomed.

My pre-war Ford Prefect benefitted greatly that week from the set of spark plugs I purchased from two young boys who had charge of a wayside petrol station. It ran better, started better and sounded better than before. On my homeward journey I picked up a young National Service soldier outside Cirencester. He was hoping for a lift as far as London but was glad to remain with me as I followed the North Circular to Essex. My final destination was Brentwood and my passenger was dropped in the High Street there. I had to be at Warley for work the following day.

One memorable week I hired a Morris Minor and drove us to stay with my brother John in Kirkcaldy. I was then married and living in Lancashire. Early in the year when I ordered the car, it was to be an Austin A40 but that was exchanged for the Morris by Summer. Going North we crossed the Forth by the new road bridge but our return was via Edinburgh and across to Moffat before heading southwards. While staying in Fife, I was keen to visit the Scottish Gliding Union by Portmoak and we followed that by walking up West Lomond and from the top of this could see the first snow that winter on the distant mountains. John's Father-in-Law, Harold Young, was also visiting them that week. Our homeward journey involved a long and unfortunate delay owing to the work of extending the M6 beyond Carnforth.

At BTR, one end of the Roller Covering workshop had a number of steam pans in which the compound was cured before it was machined. These horizontal cylindrical pans were formerly used to cure the compound of motor tyres when BTR had been the British Tyre and Rubber company. I joined them when it had become British Thermoplastics and Rubber, engineers in rubber. Distant again from gardening as both were from Plessey's electronics. My lack of learning at school was being compensated for in my working life. And more was to come. I had no experience of lathe work but I had been a skilled grinder. To "toolroom standard".

My background of fine grinding appeared to more than qualify me for consideration to become an operator on one of the BTR machines. The obvious machine for me was the big Armstrong Walmsley grinder which was in very poor condition. A previous employee had permitted deep grooves to be worn into the bed through lack of lubrication and extremely heavy granite rolls seemed to be working the machine into its grave. One of only two built by Sir W. G. Armstrong-Whitworth to a design by Walmsley this seemed to be the only grinder capable of handling the massive granite rolls. Quarried in Aberdeenshire, they were shipped to Sweden to be fitted with a steel journal at each end before final grinding on the BTR machine.

BTR were accepting no more of these granite rolls, so I did not have such work which each took about a fortnight of day and night grinding. Nothing so weighty came my way but for actual size the big suction rolls were still accepted. I surely mastered the Armstrong Walmsley machine even though at least one of our bosses strongly doubted that I could do it. He asked me the name of the grinder I used previously and refused to believe me when I told him it was a Fortuna, of which he seemed not to have heard. Yet he had scoured Europe for information regarding a new grinder. They were using a Skoda lathe which had a 6' faceplate and a waist-high bed on which the operator walked up and down.

The Armstrong Walmsley grinder had its bed at floor level and deep grooves worn therein would easily hide a few matchsticks. We were told that the 40 ton SWL crane cost thirty shillings when driven the length of our workshop. There was also a 20 ton SWL crane which we operated from the floor by push buttons but this was temperamental. Only the big crane was capable of heavy work. BTR were then opening a new factory at Glenrothes in Fife and therefore our department was gradually running down. But before the end I managed to make history. In no way could I claim it my doing alone but I was the one to benefit.

All our jobs had a time and we were paid bonus rates according to our performance. The big bronze suction rolls were a major task and many hours were allotted to each of the different operations. Before grinding they were turned on the Skoda lathe to lessen the time for grinding. We knew that one of these suction rolls was on the shop and prepared ourselves for some healthy bonus. It seemed that this one would be turned and installed in the big Armstrong Walmsley on our day shift. My opposite number on the following night shift would therefore be expecting to benefit from my labours. I could completely finish the job but if it was still at the grinder the next shift could claim up to half of the total allotted time.

The Skoda operator made an excellent job of the trimming. The crane and crew were free at just the right time. And the big roll was removed from the lathe and installed at the grinder for me to set up and begin the job. We used large wooden-framed micrometers to check the roll diameter and that afternoon I contacted the Inspector to pass the roll as completed. Then, like a miracle of timing, the crane and crew arrived at my end of the shop and the roll was promptly removed! Arthur Johnson would be coming in for the night shift fully expecting to book several hours work on that job.

The time for grinding these big rolls was about fifteen or sixteen hours. There was no disputing the fact that I had it installed, set up, ground satisfactorily and taken away within a single working shift. Next day a delegation of bosses visited me at the machine with a proposition. Either the time and motion people would be brought in and such work re-timed. Or I must book longer than a single 8-hour shift on it. I owed Arthur Johnson no loyalty and he would do nothing to benefit me. I had therefore an easy choice and all in the shop rejoiced with me. The record time was mine and also the resulting bonus.

Knowing that our Department at BTR was running down, I began looking for alternative work By this time we had a second son. My mother came up from Essex to care for Barbara while I was working and Stephen was born when I was on nightshift. The Preston Labour Exchange or Job Centre, whatever it was then called had a notice regarding a vacancy for landscape gardeners on good wages. That was for Barton Grange Garden Centre between Preston and Garstang, on the bus route to Lancaster. But I still had my bike and was fit enough to cycle there. BGGC took me on and I seemed to fit in.

Cycling between Cinnamon Hill and Leyland used more minor roads with lighter traffic apart from a section of the A6 and part of the A49. Nothing more dramatic than when I crossed the River Lostock and witnessed it frozen over in 1963. But the route north to Barton Grange meant crossing Preston. The centre of Preston was as though I had to fight a way through. Once I was beaten. Riding from Stanley Street in front of the prison, a car on my right turned left into Church St across my bows. My bike was unharmed but I was forced off and fell heavily, resulting in a lump like a goose egg swelling on my head. The driver – a stranger from North London – said he would buy me a drink but the Pubs were closed. I could not see clearly to write his particulars and offered my notebook where he put his details.

The concussion resulted in hazy vision. I cycled on and continued trying to read car licence plates. These became clearer with each mile but on reaching Barton Grange, Eddie Topping decided to take me for an x-ray. No bones were broken but I was hardly fit to work. Mr Topping was a fair boss. We knew his father during the war when he bought fruit from Grandpa's orchard. Calling with his horse-drawn van, Pete used to call him the toffee man. Mr Topping senior once took me for a ride in his Jaguar car of the type used by TV detectives.

My previous experience made the boss put me in charge of the shrubs which, like most of the stock, was all container grown. When winter came, I had the greenhouse boilers to supervise and found these could be tricky. I could set the flues according to the expected conditions but the wind might change during the night. A few times I found the fire had burnt out when unattended and a hasty relighting was called for. The following year my responsibilities were changed. The landscape crew had vehicles solely for their use and an extra van was purchased to set up a Garden Maintenance Department. This was to be my responsibility.

On Sundays in summer I had to take a turn at manning the Garden Centre alone. Opening the lock-up shop, taking responsibility for the till, the greenhouses, watering, et cetera. Besides trees, shrubs, flowers and bedding plants, we sold complete water gardens. Pre-formed plastic pools stood behind the shop and when moving a heavy hose one afternoon, I stepped backwards and the edge of a water-filled pool caught me behind the knees. The water was not particularly cold, being in the sun all day but it was very wet — as were my trousers. Fortunately we were not busy just then and the well-stocked greenhouses provided sufficient shelter. In one greenhouse I quickly removed and wrung out my jeans without being observed. After putting them back on, I returned to my duties.

The two main departments of Barton Grange Garden Centre were the containerised plant and shop sales section and the landscaping and garden design people. These had two very good foremen in Jim and Ron who seemed to be in permanent positions. I had a van of tools, an electric hedge-trimmer, lawnmower, wheeled sprayer and other equipment according to the season. I had a book of customers with garden maintenance contracts and other quite regular customers who preferred to be billed according to work completed.

Those having annual maintenance contracts sometimes argued about the time spent but my difficult job was to satisfy all the customers and my employer. Another responsibility might be supervising a young assistant. I found moody teenagers did not always favour the work.

Finding myself in a seeming groove with a great deal of responsibilty but practically no opportunity for advancement, I began to feel and to show my dissatisfaction. My attitude could have an unsettling effect on other staff and Eddie Topping and I came to agree that I should move on. We agreed a date to terminate my employment and until then I continued with the work. At the end of my final week with nothing in view, I happened to be conducting a customer around our standard trees. I always loved to sell, it did not matter what. One of my colleagues once said, "Philip would sell his own grandmother" which was only a slight exaggeration.

I knew all our trees and mentioned the advantages of various varieties. Informing the customer that the most attractive could be slow growing, he expressed a desire for quick growing varieties. He had bought a cottage next to a mixed farm which had a breeding pen of pigs within a few yards of his new home. He wanted trees around his garden to screen his home from the farm. Although this was my final morning at BGGC I retained my loyalty besides my love of selling and sold him a good number of standard trees including at least one of all our Acer varieties except the ornamental Acer brilliantissima.

This gentleman knew little about gardening and he was hoping to find someone to plant his trees. I told him I was leaving Barton Grange that morning and agreed to work for him. His derelict cottage had been unoccupied for many years and to construct a garden from this untidy, overgrown site was a challenge. I began by saying I would need a mattock and advised him to buy a sack of John Innes base fertilizer to give the new trees a good start. The previous occupant of the cottage at Howick Cross may have been an Authoress but that could have been as much as fifty years past.

Compared with my preceding employment at the busy Garden Centre at Barton Grange and before then at the BTR Works in Leyland and Farington, this place at Howick Cross was rather remote and lonely. I could see down to the Ribble where ships at times might be travelling to and from Preston dock on the tidal river. And in the other direction I have seen the farmer's wife in the road with a pitchfork because the bull was loose with some heifers in the yard. To my knowlege he never ascaped. But it was certainly a quiet and lonely place.

I planted the trees and skimmed off the tussocky turf over a wide area intending to have a lawn surrounded by shrubs and trees in a wavy-edged border. My new employer asked what I intended doing with all the rough grass, roots and all. I told him I would burn it if he permitted me to use a clump of dead bushes and small trees as a fire bottom. I used a dumper truck left by some builders to barrow all the spoil to one place. One unforgettable job I had to do there concerned a half broken Welsh pony. He had never been shod and I had to hold him the first time for the farrier. (Called a blacksmith in Lancashire.) That pony really frightened me as I fell in the straw with his forehooves raised above me. It seemed that a strong angel was guarding me.

The boss's son-in-law at Lytham wanted his overgrown garden tidied. I was loaned a mini-van for two weeks for the journey and decided that two-stage flame gunning would be the best way to manage all the overgrowth. Before I could go over it for the second burning, I lost the job. Then after five months of hard work and cycling daily between Cinnamon Hill and Howick Cross, Mr Taylor told me he could take over his own gardening. I never went back to see how he was managing but I was working at Lytham when the TSR2 experimental aircraft took off. A magnificent sight. Like a white paper dart trailing a plume of black smoke as it headed out over the sea.

BTR were recruiting and I was in need of another job. It was stressed that my previous job at Roller Covering was unavailable and I was already aware it had been moved to Scotland. If BTR would take me on in other work, I was willing to try most things. I attended for Interview and a vacancy in Fork Lift truck driving was offered. Soon I was under careful supervision and training in the Wire Stores. Space there was extremely limited and manouvering the truck while lifting heavy loads was excellent training. Following this I was driving a bigger truck in the open in a variety of tasks. We had Coventry Climax electric fork lifts.

Since I had left the roller-covering and returned to gardening, a new mixing shop had been opened at the BTR Farington works and with the fork lift truck I had to provide the transport. Mineral oil is a major constituent of rubber compounds and unloading oil drums from lorries became a frequent job. The drums were stacked horizontally on stillages in the open air. Other constituents arrived in bulk bins which were also transported by fork lift truck. While I was absent for some ear surgery, a change of procedure in the mixing shop meant that bulk bins of carbon black were being installed and untied by the truck driver. This I refused to do. Without ear drums and an open fistula behind one ear, I considered the risk to my health inadvisable. In my youth I had been advised to avoid dusty conditions.

The management were not pleased with my decision but I was still young and felt I must avoid any behaviour detrimental to my health. This meant yet a further change of job. My two previous jobs with BTR were at the Farington, Centurion Way, group of factories. This third job was in Leyland. At Centurion Way the departments were widely spaced with grassed areas and wide roads between. And all were single storey. The Leyland works I audibly described as having been built for horse-drawn carts. With a long narrow yard and every department crammed into fairly compact spaces. Low doorways and ceilings, narrow passages and all crowded closely together made it a quite testing job for us drivers.

I worked in so many stores jobs, it could seem confusing. The actual General Stores was on the top floor with wooden stairways up from the yard. We stocked tools such as knives, gloves, brats and brushes. I felt the need to argue that some were brooms. A foreman said one item was a sweeping brush and I insisted it was a broom. Life in Lancashire is very unlike anything I was used to. Brats are what we call aprons. We had paper too. Sheets of greaseproof paper were stocked for the cooks and canteens. Toast was a major item in Lancashire factories, perhaps inherited from the cotton mills of old. A 'toast boy' collected orders from the canteen to be delivered to his customers in greaseproof paper.

The fork lift truck driving I had been doing came under the Stores division. At the Leyland works I still drove fork lifts but other responsibilities were added. The rubber stores was kept quite warm and cosy for storing the bales of smoked sheet and occasionally bales of crepe rubber too. Delivered to us by flat bed articulated lorry, the bales looked quite similar to concrete blocks. All the stores workers had to be involved in off-loading the heavy bales, barrowing them in and stacking them under the low ceiling. Large silverfish scurried around on the warm floor.

China clay was delivered by the ton in paper sacks which were laid out on wooden pallets. The fork truck was of course involved in this but some deliveries required careful man-handling. Nitrogen cylinders were always moved by hand. Carbon Black came in a number of types, some in sacks and some in bulk bins but at Leyland with too little space for bins it had all to be in sacks. The Black Store was dimly lit and sacks could be damaged with their contents spilling onto the floor. New responsibility came my way when I was upgraded to take on the Oil and Solvents stores.

Rubber solutions of various kinds were mixed on site and most used either petroleum spirit or toluene. Other types came in drums or barrels but toluene and petroleum were delivered by road tankers and stored in large tanks shielded by brick walls. I would be warned when a bulk delivery was coming and had to be available when the tanker arrived. I had a steam-driven donkey pump to off-load the tanker into one or other of our large tanks. Tanker deliveries (1000 gallons of petroleum, or 2000 of toluene) were not solely my responsibilty. Someone from the laboratory had also to be involved. A small quantity collected in a glass jar was tested in the lab to ascertain the correct product was being delivered and it could be quite alarming to watch the clear liquid evaporating over a bunsen flame.

Regular deliveries of fabric for the cloth store were delivered by a Courtaulds van from Bocking. The driver told me he would be glad to take me to Essex if ever I wanted to go. Barbara and I then had two boys and I formed a plan or at least a wish to return to our native Essex for her father to enjoy his only grandchildren. Mr Merry had lung trouble with part of one removed. This may have been through his work as a Printer's Colour Mixer with quantities of carbon black involved over many years. His sudden death came as a shock to us all.

Five years previously we had been holidaying in Essex when our third son was stillborn. Out for a walk with my father one time, we returned to hear that Barbara had been rushed to hospital in Billericay. I caught the next bus there but found the journey was in vain. Unfortunately, Barbara did not feel able to discuss matters with me but the young doctor told me it was no one's fault. Our baby may have died before we left Lancashire. It was a second shock to us all, especially to Stephen who seemed to have appointed himself as the expected baby's guardian.

The unexpected death of Barbara's father affected us all. Her mother was crippled with arthritis and it seemed right for us to help her. Alan, our fourth son was born shortly after the passing of the grandfather he never knew. By then new classrooms had been built at Severn Drive School and Stephen had finally started there. Elder brother Philip had started when the school was newly opened with plenty of space for children to start young. But Stephen's eventual start was delayed until extra class rooms were added. I felt it best to leave my job with BTR and start yet another new life in Essex. I gave in my notice to quit when the Summer break came and arranged with the Courtauld's driver to travel down with him.

Jock picked me up from home before he made a delivery to a shop in Church St Preston. He made other deliveries including one or two in Wigan. We made a night stop in Leek at the Premier Dye Works. Jock knew his way around and took me for a meal before we bedded down at the Dye Works, a part of the Courtauld Group. He slept as he usually did in the cab of the van after bringing out large bundles of rags to make a soft bed in the back for me. The roller shutter at the rear of the van was left up all night and I witnessed a vivid thunderstorm, reminiscent of the one I had watched over Chelmsford Viaduct from hospital in 1948.

Next morning we returned the rags into the mill and set off south. We were delayed by a gigantic load on a low trailer that pulled out before us in leaving a transport café. I watched an operator on a footplate steering the rear axles. My driver understood that I had relatives in Brentwood and Barbara had her widowed mother near Maldon. As we journeyed on, he suggested dropping me near Bishops Stortford for onward travel to Brentwood or in Dunmow where I could go down to Maldon. I refused both these suggestions. God had been speaking to me. My destination was to be Braintree.

Jock was aware that I had no contacts in Braintree. I remembered once passing through the town on an ROC day out to Stradishall Aerodrome but had never set foot in the town. But God had reminded me of our former life in Ingatestone. In the 1940s, the Elim church at Ingatestone had a visit from a preacher who cycled over from Bocking Church Street. His name was Harry

Clark and like most visiting preachers, he came to our home for lunch. He came more than once and my parents became friends with Mr Clark. We got to know some of his family, his daughter Ruth and son John. John Clark liked to call my brother John "Johnny".

Because of God's prompting I was determined to be taken to Braintree. Jock knew of nowhere I could be sure of a bed for the night but God knew. I asked to be dropped at the Police station where I would make enquiries. This may or may not have been God's intention but I know I make mistakes. The Police officer at Fairfield Road was no help. He would not even allow me to leave my bags and boots there. It seemed quite a climb up Fairfield Road but I soon came to the Eastern National bus office where I asked for a Left Luggage department. I was directed to the nearby Council Bus Park where the Council employee took in my belongings for three old pence (3d).

I told this Council man at the Bus Park I thought I could get help through anyone in the Elim church. There would surely be an Elim church because of our contact with Harry Clark. The Council employee sent me to find Martin's Yard where I would find a John Anderson. Martin's Yard, between Braintree High St and Coronation Avenue was the Council depot where they had their stores and the dustcarts were kept. John Anderson was obviously an Elim member besides a Council storeman. He immediately phoned his pastor who gave him instructions for me. I was to catch a certain bus to "The Lillies" in Bocking Church Street and find Harry and Mrs Clark who had a Council house close by.

My arriving to announce myself at the front door must have surprised them. Being country people, the Clarks would most times use the back door. After a pause for breath, Mr Clark said, "Well, you'd better come in, we take all the waifs and strays". They had recently given accomodation to a young lady from Sri Lanka and for two nights I slept in the spare room that she had used. Harry Clark was going to see an elderly man in Boleyn's Avenue that evening to cut his hair before he went away for a holiday. Knowing I needed work and hoped to buy a house Mr Clark directed me to find both the Job Centre in Panfield Lane and the town centre for Estate agents.

Crossing the Council Estate I soon found the Job Centre and went on to locate Estate agents in town. I could see nothing more definate to be done that evening and returned to my new friends in Church Street. When the Job Centre opened, the young man noted my previous experience driving forklift trucks and was pleased to find a vacancy advertised in the local weekly. Unfortunately, that position had already been filled. The Fertilizer Depot in Railway St apologised for their advertisement appearing in the latest edition of the Braintree and Witham Times. It was a mistake. That job was taken a week previously.

A lternative employment might well be with a new business in the district. The Emerald Furniture Company were recruiting trainee upholsterers in preparation for their new factory to be opened. New workers were being trained and interviews conducted at temporary premises in Victoria Street beside the Council Bus Park where my stay in Braintree had begun. This was my next destination. The Emerald Foreman was conducting interviews while giving training to a few new employees. He expressed a keen interest in my training as a storeman and told me they had not previously employed one. Before leaving the Clarks, I found that they listened to Trans World Radio each morning on a large radiogram.

I was to await the opening of the new Emerald factory on the Springwood Estate and then to reapply. They had no date for this and therefore I decided to spend the time helping my own position. One need was for personal transport. My parents accomodated me in Brentwood where I bought a Honda 50 motorcycle. Before leaving BTR I had given up cycling as advised by the ENT consultant and was relieved of both my bikes by a fellow forklift truck driver, Marshal Higginbotham. I considered that the speed differential between my cycling and motor traffic contributed to the hazard. Subsequent experience proved this to be an oversimplified view. I could and did fall from a motorcycle.

For work at the Emerald Furniture factory I was travelling to Braintree daily from the cottage where Barbara's mother lived between Hazeleigh and Maldon. This being not to her convenience we made it a Monday to Friday arrangement. The few weekends I did stay at the cottage, I quite enjoyed meeting with the Maldon Elim Church. Otherwise I rode my Honda to stay with my brother David in Canning Town. During the time I worked for Mr Lesley Cater, our Dave had a sudden misfortune. After his Army service, he had worked on the railway at

Bishopsgate to save up to marry his Intended. They were engaged before his National Service.

For a few brief months David had worked on another farm to obtain a tied cottage. His wife, Miriam, expired through influenza after nine months marriage and Dave was evicted from the cottage for being unwed. Hearing of this Mr Cater asked to see my brother, as he knew local farmers who might be willing to employ Dave. Anyone seeing my big brother might offer him work because of his physique and pleasant manner. As when Willie Steven already had his vacancy filled at Master John's farm when Dave applied but took him on because, at fifteen years, he was bigger and stronger than many mature men. He would work like a man for a boy's wage.

Soon after meeting Mr Cater, David was working at Cater Bros store in Romford. He then married again and was offered a Caretaker's job at Caters Supermarket in Canning Town. That was where I spent weekends with David and Christina. Some weekends I would be with Barbara and our boys at our home in Walton-le-Dale. Travelling back and forth on overnight buses was not ideal but we trusted it would not be for long. Emerald Furniture had promised a good rate of pay following initial training. But we learned later that to get that amount would be when we could each complete a three-piece suite per day.

This was never going to happen in my case because after my initial training I worked in the Stores. I insisted that the promise of good pay included me, but they said it was for production workers and I was non-productive. I therefore deserted Emerald, deliberately leaving the stores disorganised and taking another job driving a forklift truck and a Bedford TK lorry. My new job with Vernon Marsh engineers was a great impovement where I felt appreciated. Most of their production was for Lake and Elliot Jacks and I was frequently driving to the Lake and Elliot works with pallets of 2-ton bottle jacks intended for Transit vans. Other subcontract work was taken on and my work included driving to a number of factories around Colchester besides to Hayters at Spellbrook and Ransomes at Ipswich.

While with Marsh I was planning to obtain night work which might permit me to go jobbing gardening in daylight. Word came that Courtaulds at Bocking were planning a Night Shift for loading their vans at the five-storey building and I applied for this. Vernon Marsh found that the heavy steering on his Bedford TK had been caused by previous damage. After having this repaired he could more easily drive the lorry himself. So my leaving him caused him no great hardship and I settled to regular night work at Courtaulds. I slept part of each day Monday to Friday and was busy in other things on Saturdays after night-shift.

I had by then become a member of Black Notley Mission and attended their weeknight meetings before going on to work. My little Honda was well used although I never rode it to Lancashire. This regular night work at Courtaulds brought about the greatest change ever in my life. Backing up the vans of varying size to the loading dock became routine and I quite enjoyed doing that besides being part of the team loading up. We stacked the rolls of fabric in the specified order and parked the vans by the riverside across the yard. Other times we made up parcels for despatch.

On Saturday 10th March 1973 after working the night shift, I took our eldest boy Philip Edmund, to see his Grandparents in Brentwood. It was late and growing dark when we left there and rode away. As usual, I avoided the A12 and took a cross-country route by way of Ongar road and Blackmore. Somewhere in the Kelvedon Hatch region, I somehow lost my seating and ended up unconscious at the roadside. Philip was then twelve years old and on that dark evening he had the presence of mind to try getting help. Rather than a single car, I learned later that perhaps as many as three cars had stopped for us.

The local Police constable was also involved besides the Emergency Ambulance. Young Philip told me later that he was given the choice to go with me to hospital or not. Being only 12 years old with a painful wound to his knee he could hardly stay there alone, miles from home. We were taken to Harold Wood Hospital where Philip had two stitches put in a minor leg wound. Still unconscious at the A&E department, I was checked over, x-rayed and then transferred to a Mens Surgical Ward where I was to remain for six weeks. Barbara came with the Salvation Army officer from Braintree to take Philip home. Lieutenant Stan Skelton was an excellent neighbour.

My condition over the following three weeks remains something of a mystery. One of the other patients told me later that I had chatted with them at the meal table but I had no recollection of that. It was as though I was asleep. I do not know how I reached the table but when I became fully conscious I had a wheelchair to move around in. Waking up in a hospital bed was nothing new for me. From my previous experiences, I knew that hospital bed linen and drapes normally had a sewn in name for the laundry. Within my reach I found Harold Wood Hospital sewn in red thread. So I would be in there.

Fully conscious I may have been but whether sane or otherwise was in some doubt. I had visitors of course and some interaction with other patients. Harold Wood and Brentwood being only one train station apart my mother would most likely have been a frequent visitor. She could walk to Brentwood Station from her house and the hospital was a short walk from Harold Wood station. My brother Peter cheered me up and he seemed to enjoy being there. Gordon Lincoln also came in but one regular visitor was a complete stranger. My weird waking-sleeping state made me unaware of different days or times and I cannot say when this stranger first spoke to me. But I do remember him once asking whether I knew him. It was an afternoon when Peter had been in to sit with me.

The white-haired stranger sat beside me as I lay in bed. "Do you know me" he asked, and I replied "Is it Uncle Tom"? To his denial I said "I have got an uncle Tom" remembering my father's brother who was white haired and ruddy faced like this elderly man. My visitor told me he had been seeing me each week as he visited every patient in that Ward. He was a Christian and belonged to the Christian Brethren denomination. God had once healed him of a brain haemorrhage in that same Ward. Since then he visited there regularly and moreover he prayed nightly on his knees for every bed on that Ward.

He remarked about the Bible on my bedside locker. Barbara had brought in the paperback edition of the Good News Bible in Today's English which I had been reading to our boys Philip and Stephen when they were in bed. The boys were quite interested in Old Testament stories. Stephen once commented "They keep having wars". When, in the twentieth Psalm I read, "Some trust in chariots and some in horses" Philip said that he liked Fire Engines best. Although in later years he much preferred Grand Prix racing cars in their place.

B efore leaving me my elderly visitor quietly prayed with his mouth close to my ear, that God would bless, heal and restore me. A simple and childlike helpful prayer which really did me good. My white-haired visitor made clear his disapproval of that attractively covered Good News Bible. In his opinion it should have a black cover and contain the King James Version. But there in Harold Wood Hospital in 1973 my infantile condition kept me from reading anything beyond The Perishers strip cartoon in someone's Paper. Even so, God was helping me. When I told the old man how much I enjoyed his prayer, he replied, "Brother, I always pray like that". Earlier he had told me I should not call him "Mate". But we should always call each other "Brother". And I told him my brother had been in that chair and I had called him "mate". As we used to do as boys.

Y et to me the old man's childlike prayers and his preferred version of the bible did not agree. In my simple state I asked why, if he could pray that way, "Why must the Bible be all thees, thous and verilies"? My loving visitor had no answer to this. God was helping me, I am sure. Far beyond this experience were nightly visits when all was quiet and the lights were low. Anyone with experience of being an Inpatient will remember the lights being reduced for patients to sleep and the Night staff to go quietly about their duties. Quite often though, they do little going about but sit knitting.

T his was the time the Lord Jesus used to come to my bedside. I felt rather than saw Him beside me. First he told me that my being there was no accident. Being struck unconscious on that road was in his plan for my life. On three consecutive evenings I heard Him speaking to me. He said he approved of my Christian life but wanted my manner to change. I had been reading the Bible, praying to God, even as best I could teaching in Sunday School. "That was all well and good," he said "but do it for pleasure." "Get some fun from it." I had been doing these things as my duty, believing that was the proper way to be a Christian.

T he Lord Jesus knew all about me. He knew that I am (or was) stubborn, resisting changes. He showed me how he wanted to change my fixed way to conform to his way. As though bending a straight object to align it with a gentle corrugation. "Relax" he said, "Relax". "If a baby lies still in his mother's arms he is perfectly safe", I heard. "But if he kicks and struggles, she could drop him." If I learned only one thing over those three evenings of lessons, I must relax, not be so stubborn and unbending.

And what a Teacher! As a Private Tutor He showed me pictures as though using a card index inside my head. This was in 1973, remember. It might now seem more like a datafile or even colour slides. Three times my Lord picked out a film clip or video to show me. He wanted to make my stubborn will conform to His holy will. Being so stiff, this bending my will to conform to his was going to be a painful process. Quite unpleasant but my acceptance was truly rewarding. Deep joy followed each time as His loved flowed in. I knew little or nothing about teaching but Jesus used visual aids in his lessons.

If and when I accepted His offer, I knew the joy of obedience. A hard case like me would take hard lessons. My Teacher showed me three pictures. Whether these were on one evening or spread over three, after so many years I cannot recall. First I was shown a clip with me being a great idler along with young children. Our son Alan was then under school age and I might at first be sharing life with him and be always with children of a similar age. Not an attractive prospect, when I might well expect to return to Samuel Courtauld at Bocking.

Looking at this daunting scene of future life as no more than a five-year-old, I shrank from it. But feeling the love of the Lord Jesus alongside me, I relaxed and told him, "If that is truly your plan for me, yes Lord, I would accept that." Immediately, my Lord reassured me that I would not have to face such a future and his love flowed over and into me. His next scene was more daunting than the first. I saw what would probably have been a Victorian Insitution with redbrick walls surrounded by green painted railings. This had to be a place of committal for a lifetime with no possibility of release.

What a fearful picture! Confined to bed at that late hour I had no way of escape. I felt forced to face up to the prospect. While being tormented by these fearsome scenes, my Lord must have given me inner strength to survey and consider it. At last I drew strength enough to say again, "If that is truly your will for me, yes Lord, I would accept even that." Immediately, once again my Lord reassured me with his loving answer. "No, son, I love you and have better things for you than that." And his love again flowed over and into me.

Such Insitutions may no longer exist in this 21st Century but in 1973 two men in white coats came to examine and test me there in Harold Wood Hospital. I had something of an upset the night before and poor Barbara was told I'd had a brainstorm – whatever that may have been. I was in a private side room when these two came in. The one with a beard did the speaking while the other listened, perhaps taking notes. For weeks I had had extreme double vision and could see nothing clearly. This added to the general feeling of sleep-walking.

"Tell me about your work" said the bearded one. My work was many miles distant and of no seeming importance to anyone there in the hospital. So I replied, "No, let's talk about your work". "My work is to ask you these questions", he replied. I immediately relaxed, slumping down on the pillows and telling him something like, "Okay, ask me whatever you want". My most recent work was at Samuel Courtauld, loading the big vans in the riverside yard at Bocking. My remarks must have satisfied the two strangers and they soon left me. I never saw either of them again but guessed they were from Severalls Mental Hospital.

For my next test, even more forbidding, I saw myself lying supinely at the bottom of somewhere deep. In this my Teacher had the laugh on me. He knew that as a child I had discussed with my mother the depth to which graves were dug. "Six feet under" was a common enough saying but in cities I was told, they are often twenty feet deep. "There you are at the bottom", Jesus said. "Six feet or twenty does not matter now, there you are at the bottom with no way out." I saw feet above me. Boots moving up and down as I watched. Treading the soil back in place permanently. Surely not! When well I saw myself as a working man.

A corpse? Me? Down through the years of illness and accidents; stretchers and ambulances; I had always returned alive and kicking. Returning eventually to school or to whichever job I had at the time. But condemned to an early grave so unexpectedly, no! I could not face that. But face it I must. Jesus coming to my bedside, showing me these pictures and asking me to choose, required me to look carefully and come to a decision. Twice before I had found his testing almost too much to take but had finally accepted what I understood was his will for me. And I trusted Him as a friend.

Now, watching these boots above me, was frightening and I could not turn away. The picture was for me alone and I must choose. Not something to be rushed but considered carefully. For the third time Jesus asked me, "If that is my plan for you, would you accept that." I had no doubt of my Lord's love. Jesus and his love are inseparable. His love surrounded me, I could feel it and he was there awaiting my decision. Finally I drew enough courage to say "If that is truly your will for me, yes Lord, I would accept that." For a third time his love flowed over and into me in even greater abundance. And instantly I had His reassuring answer. "No, son, I have better for you than that."

I felt so overjoyed, I wanted to rush out and throw my arms around everyone to hug them. But I had no mobilty other than a wheelchair and could not leave the Ward. My Lord had worked on me with so much patience till I had agreed to even death. I knew his promise of eternal life, I had read it so many times. As Jesus said to Martha, sister of Lazarus, "I am the resurrection and the life. He who believes in me will live even if he dies; and no one who lives and believes in me will ever die. Do you believe this?" Martha believed it and I believed it. Apart from believing and trusting, I had done nothing. But I heard Jesus tell me, "No, son, I will give you more years with Barbara and the boys." He told me the Bible would seem like a new book and my prayers would be a genuine pleasure.

Never before had I known such emotion in me. So much love that I would have rushed outside to throw my arms round everyone and anyone I met. That is if I was on my feet. But I had only a wheelchair to move around in when I was out of bed. It was then my Lord promised me more years of life with Barbara and the boys. But that must be sometime in the future. Still hospitalised with post concussive effects and no indication of how much longer I would remain there, I had to obey the Doctors' instructions.

For the first three weeks there I would have been barely conscious. When I began to become aware of myself and life around me, the doctors knew my condition required careful treatment. They had to explain things to me as to a young child. It was explained that I would not have to fear any kind of treatment. I would merely be taken to Oldchurch Hospital for "Tests" twice in one week. No treatment, they stressed, only tests. So on Monday and

Thursday of the following week I was taken by wheelchair from my bed to an ambulance waiting outside. A sitting type ambulance with clear windows.

This would be perhaps a month after the emergency 999 ambulance had taken me to Harold Wood Hospital, unconscious. And still I was barely conscious. Severe double vision, seeing nothing clearly gave the effect of sleep walking. From Harold Wood we went along Eastern Avenue which was a chain of roundabouts. As the ambulance negotiated each one, I was watching in expectation of a collision. Not expecting another vehicle to collide with the ambulance but that I would be struck and woken from sleep. It would be as though I awoke suddenly from a vivid nightmare to find myself on the floor beside my bed in Braintree. A waking dream.

Arriving safely at Oldchurch Hospital the ambulance crew asked to which department they were to take me. I sleepily mumbled something and they realised I was going for EEG, Electro Encephalogram. I was wheeled into a room where a young girl began gluing wires to my head. When a web of fine flexible wires had been glued all over my head, the girl sat at a console or keyboard and began giving me instructions. "Open your eyes, shut your eyes" she repeated as I sat in trepidation, genuinely fearing that she intended to kill me. While I had this feeling of consternation, it merely seemed part of the ongoing dream of the time.

If I was killed it was only a dream anyway and waking next morning always brings escape from whatever the dream might be. In childhood I had two recurring nightmares which troubled me perhaps for years but each faded on waking. Having been a hospital patient so frequently both in childhood and later, to be dreaming of such events as these appeared normal. I may even have slept on the return journey to Harold Wood Hospital. Monday's "Test" was over but there was still Thursday to come. Once again, I was wheeled out to a sitting type ambulance with clear windows.

Again the drive to and through Romford. On arrival this time my wheelchair was pushed into a waiting room. There may have been one or two other patients waiting and there seemed to be an aquarium with live fish. Nothing was clearly seen with my continuing double vision. After what seemed only a brief wait, I was taken to a small side room or laboratory. The man who wheeled me there held my bared arm while his partner prepared a hypodermic injection. Then came something difficult to relate and impossible to understand. No dream this time but a life changing event.

To have a hypodermic needle pushed into me was nothing new and nothing remarkable but for the fact that instantly, a new life was begun within me. There I sat with two unknown men for an unexplained event. In fact, this incident in the small side room was to prepare me for my next "Test" which was to be with a second young woman. But that was still future. Even before the "hypo" was used to inject whatever it was, as the needle point went through the skin of my arm, three definate and distinct phenomena occurred.

Being struck across one's nape with a 3 inch fence post I imagine would be similar to this occurence. Three distinct but simultaneous happenings. A flash of yellow light at the back of my eyes; a loud bang inside my ears; and a heavy blow to the back of my neck. There may also have been a baby's whimper from my lips. But nothing actually happened apart from a sharp needle piercing the skin of my forearm. One immediate result was that my dream-like vision cleared. For the first time in some weeks I had clear sight and watched as the man with the hypodermic withdrew the plunger. This puzzled me.

Never before had I seen this done but years later someone kindly explained that the subsequent drawing up of blood was to ensure that the injection entered the correct place – a blood vessel. With my newly restored eyesight I watched, fascinated. I felt wideawake after weeks of a dreamlike existence and the fresh red blood looked more beautiful than anything I'd ever seen. I was then wheeled back to the waiting room and yes, there was an aquarium with live fish. Now I could see clearly and the colourful fish looked beautiful. The other patients had gone and I was happy to sit watching these colourful tropical fish. I learnt later that probably they were from Lake Malawi.

Whatever had been injected into my bloodstream evidently took time to circulate but after some time had elapsed I was taken to another room for the second 'Test'. Unlike the EEG previously when I thought the young person intended to kill me this was a quite pleasant experience. Out of the wheelchair and onto a form or table top I had to lie with my head supported by a stirrup-like bracket. My eyesight was still somewhat faulty and I misjudged the distance, almost catching my right eye on the bracket. The young lady technician apologised for this lack of care on her part. She also apologised for what she would be using being "a noisy machine".

As I lay there in the neck support two mechanical arms slid out above and below my head and then I could hear the aforementioned noise. This amused me as I mentally compared the two 'tests' for which I was sent to Oldchurch. In the first I was instructed continually to "Open your eyes, shut your eyes" and so on. Whereas in this second 'test' I was told to lie still and "Think about anything". Thinking logically, it seemed that one test depended on light and vision and the second worked by sound. This is not a noisy machine, I thought. It's a machine constructed to make an audible sound when needed. Open and closed, on and off, as required.

I could see on one wall in this young lady's room a framed picture of yachts in a bay. A colourful picture to enhance her quite pleasant room. Quite a contrast to the EEG place. Following this strange procedure I was ready to be returned to Harold Wood Hospital. In my wheelchair I was taken to another waiting room where the transport crew would collect me. There was one other patient there, a lady with a leg in plaster resting upon a bench. She was patiently knitting whereas I felt very impatient. It was past midday and I was hungry. Whenever I was in the ward at Harold Wood meals were served regularly and I never once had a feeling of hunger.

It appeared that the transport crew were taking their meal break and making us wait. I wanted to be returned to Harold Wood and have the meal I might miss. I was a bundle of emotion and anxiety with stirrings of new life. The waiting room clock, reminding me of the passing meal time was one thing. But I was also actively studying the calendar on the wall. "What year are we in? What month is it? Will we be hurrying back before my dinner is cleared away?" Too many questions flooded my thoughts without ready answers.

My anxiousness was relieved as the ambulance crew came and collected us. But the expected swift return to have my food was frustrated by one patient being taken to Collier Row before I was returned to Harold Wood Hospital. Once there I had my feet down for walking. To the ambulanceman's surprise, I refused the wheelchair saying "Oh no, I can walk". Using my hands to guide me along the passage walls and bed ends in the ward, I safely reached my bed. The man in the next bed looked up, surprised. "You're walking!" he said. "Yes, I've walked all the way back from Oldchurch", I replied, cheekily.

Refusing to accept the fact that mealtime had passed, I fussed and insisted that an alternative be provided. Before long a tasty cold salad was brought to me by a nurse and I thoroughly enjoyed it. In fact salad became a real favourite from then on. Visitors had left me a bowl of fruit. Peeling an orange seemed too difficult but later on I managed to consume a banana. Before long I developed a nettle-rash across my chest at which the Ward Sister appeared to take fright. She instructed a nurse to go over my chest with calamine lotion on cotton wool. I felt no discomfort but they were worried only about the appearance, not any possibility of pain.

I was learning to manage without the wheelchair but found walking a strange experience. Judging distances and angles took some effort. Around this time something clicked at the back of my neck and my vision changed. It was as though I could see more clearly upwards rather than as previously when looking down. So by lowering my chin to my chest, seeing my way to walk was easier. This would be when they telephoned Barbara and told her my head had fallen forward. I felt the need for exercise and asked, as well as I could, for physiotherapy. They told me I must help myself without a Physiotherapist.

Feeling an urge to write, whatever I wrote turned out to be nonsense. There were books in the Dayroom but I found any attempt at reading was frustrated by my having no short-term memory. Even could I assimilate enough of a story to reach the bottom of a page, turning to the next I had to begin again. Nothing of the previous page was remembered. I might understand a strip-cartoon but nothing more. But I clearly remembered when my brother John was born in 1939. Peter then had a new toy, a clockwork steam-roller. Clicking harshly the small model ran quickly forward and reverse on the floor.

I remembered telling Pete, "Show it to the new baby" to the amusement of our mother. I meant no joke but the as yet unnamed new baby was sleeping, as always. I could remember rabbit hutches in the garden. I also remembered being lifted up to see the little locomotives climbing up the Gas

Works slag heap. They made green smoke. My earliest memory would be of the realisation that I could do or see things others could not. Sitting at the meal table in a baby's high chair, I was facing the window. Beyond the window I could see into the garden where a pole supported the clothes-line for the flat upstairs.

Cheap glass in the window caused distortion and by swaying from side to side in my chair I could cause ripples to run up and down the pole. The family wanted me to sit still but that would take away my feeling of being in control. This realisation made me feel special, different and privileged. Perhaps it was even character-forming because throughout my childhood, whenever I was ill-treated or unduly punished, I could take comfort from knowing or seeing things others could not. Being the second son, I always felt it neccessary to compete with David, the firstborn. When he was given a presentation teaspoon, I must have cried for one of my own. I was consoled by someone giving me an apostle spoon – the only one in our home.

The time for my discharge approached and the doctors told me I had received no treatment – apart from bed rest. But they were certain that as my condition improved, I must expect severe headaches, about which nothing could be done. Six weeks had passed since that fateful Saturday 10th March and on Monday 23rd April Barbara came by train to take me home. She thoughtfully used her shopping trolley to bring my heavy overcoat to keep me from getting cold. One of the nurses had helped me walk outside for fresh air but I was weak from too little activity. So my overcoat was too heavy for me to wear and it remained in the shopping trolley.

It was good to be back in Braintree and, being St George's Day, the flag was flying as we passed St Michael's church. I was happy to see it and would have liked more flags. By long tradition, parish churches fly St George's Cross on appropriate days. Barbara would have chosen a taxi to reach home but that seemed to me like defeat. But on arriving home I was tired and ready for bed. At Harold Wood Hospital the Consultant was Mr Messent, under whom my father had been admitted when his war wound became ulcerated. I do not remember the names of doctors under him but on a follow-up visit one of them told me they had no record of any fractures and I had received no treatment.

Mr Messent, a very tall, long limbed gentleman, had during WW II as I learnt later, performed an emergency appendectomy on himself. My discharge letter had begun home visits from our GP, a Dr Avery-Jones, who must have tired of writing "post concussive syndrome" on my sicknotes. At least once he noted my condition as *hair-line fracture*. Mr Messent was interested to see the name Avery-Jones on my notes. He said a Dr Avery-Jones had been Knighted for his work at the Central Middlesex Hospital. Our GP, with a light laugh, told me that this was his brother. But our doctor in Braintree had formerly specialised in tropical diseases.

Thankfully, I never had the severe headaches the doctors had warned me about. But I had no more than a three-minute attention span. Beside the bed at home I had a communications radio receiver bought a year or two previously. The expected introduction of VAT would raise the cost of these and many other things besides. Planning ahead, I had taken our boys Philip and Stephen up to London for a day to buy the new receiver. I had already decided on a Lafayette HA 600A. While my cheque was cleared, we crossed the Thames to Lambeth and spent time in the Imperial War Museum there.

One of the first things I wanted to try after leaving hospital was to discover whether I could continue my hobby of short wave radio listening. I was a member of ISWL, the International Short Wave League and Dick Whittington had encouraged me to join WACRAL The World Association of Christian Radio Amateurs and Listeners. On the Wednesday morning, only two days after coming home I tuned to the Trans World Radio signal from Monte Carlo. Normally I would have been either at work or asleep at such an hour but listening on Wednesday morning was ideal to hear the word of God. That morning I heard for the first time a Pastor Dennis Paterson on the Live a New Life weekly broadcast. Listening to Pastor Dennis, who later became a sincere friend, fulfilled my need at that time. In my 2—3 minute attention span, this man of God got through to my mind in just the way Jesus had been doing in hospital.

Barbara and I had tried several Christian denominations without finding one we found really satisfying – even the latest where I become a member at Black Notley Mission. Listening to Pastor Dennis Paterson brought the realisation that above all, we needed the great love of Jesus. Some years later at a Retreat, the Conductor expressed surprise that our experience in Pentecostal

Missions and Assemblies had not found that love. God's written word tells us that the greatest of all Spiritual gifts is love and the others are worthless without it. And listening to Pastor Dennis renewed the joy I knew when listening to the Lord Jesus himself.

Jesus had been speaking in love at my hospital bedside and at home I was hearing that same love though my radio. The Live a New Life weekly programmes on Trans World Radio included poetry recitations, choir pieces and solos besides the brief and encouraging talk by Pastor Dennis. With improving health, my attention span increased and I could listen to the full quarter-hour Live a New Life broadcasts of Pastor Dennis Paterson and the Come Back To God Campaign Team. On each Wednesday morning, the invitation was given to write to the Come Back To God Campaign. When I became well enough, I wrote to them at the announced address and have remained on their mailing list ever since I wrote back in 1973.

With improving health I was becoming increasingly active. After coming home from hospital I was visited by Dr Avery-Jones but I always I felt the need to extend myself and to do as much as I possibly could. I objected to being seen as an invalid having home visits from the doctor. So when I was due for a repeat Sick-note, I asked Alan to walk with me to the doctor's Surgery. Walking along Rayne Road past the Horse and Groom pub I felt nervous and asked Alan to hold my hand. This was some years before I regularly used a walking-stick.

Four-year-old Alan looked up, surprised and said, "I don't need to hold your hand". I had to humbly explain that my need was to hold his hand. He then willingly and perhaps proudly conducted me to the GP's surgery. Dr Avery-Jones was surprised I had made the effort but he did not rebuke me for so doing. Alan was still under school age and Barbara encouraged me to go out with him. A dairy farm not far away at Clapbridge had a public footpath through the farm yard and across the disused railway. Beyond the former railway, we could walk beside the River Brain. One time I well remember, Barbara gave me a packet of potato crisps to share with Alan. Finding the packet too difficult to open I wept, but Alan willingly and calmly came to the rescue.

The Nurse from Samuel Courtauld at Bocking visited us each week, bringing my weekly pay and doubtless checking on my state of recovery.

She once strongly encouraged me to join a group who were going by car to Courtauld's Convalescent Home at Cheltenham. I knew that I was nowhere near well enough for that and rejected her offer. I was of course thinking of myself. Realising that my state of health was placing additional burdens on Barbara, I began to reconsider Courtauld's generous offer. Apart from me, Barbara had the three boys, Philip and Stephen at school and Alan not yet begun school and she had her mother living upstairs.

I can remember at times, Barbara running into our bedroom (downstairs because our home was a semi-bungalow) and hidden, panting, in the wardrobe; like a frightened rabbit. This was her reaction to hearing her mother descending the stairs. Mother, three boys and an invalid husband day after day was too much for anyone to bear. The ongoing pressure I could see was making Barbara ill. If she could be relieved of the need to care for me for a while, that might help her. I almost regretted refusing the opportunity to attend Courtauld's Convalescent Home and decided to try that. Mentioning it to the Nurse when she came next time revealed that it was not a regular occurence.

Nurse could not say when another group would be going. I had missed the chance. But there might be another option. Courtauld's then had two Convalescent Homes. The one at Cheltenham and another at Colwyn Bay in North Wales. Arrangements were made and I was offered the chance to go to Colwyn Bay. They gave me a rail warrant for travel from Braintree to Witham and Liverpool Street and from Euston by train to Colwyn Bay. They even provided me with £5 for the taxi ride between Liverpool Street and Euston. I made the journey but was really not fit to travel alone.

At Euston mainline terminus I was helped onto the train and to a corner seat facing the direction of travel. I had to remain seated there until I could see that we were pulling into Colwyn Bay station. Two nuns sat opposite me for the whole journey from Euston. My childhood train travel sufficed to keep me calm and I was interested to note the varied sections of the route. The train was the Irish Mail from London to Holyhead and as far as Crewe it had electric propulsion at 100mph. From there as far as Chester it was Diesel hauled at 90mph. Beyond Chester the Irish Mail became a slow train stopping at most, if not all, stations. Running by the Dee estuary was unlike any of my previous rail journeys.

Alarge, brown, Mercedes taxi was waiting to convey me to Courtauld's Convalescent Home on the top of a hill with sea views. I was greeted by a friendly welcome from a man who had stayed behind while the others had all gone out for a celebration party. When they returned he introduced me as "Prince Philip without the Prince". On the Monday morning I had to see the local retained GP who had to assess all the new intake. Dr Wainwright took a genuine interest in me and I was greatly helped by talking with him. So much so that I asked to see him again the following Monday when he was there to see newcomers.

Courtauld's being such a large Group, other people were there from Wrexham [Wrecsam], Flint, Grimsby and the Midlands. I was the only one from "down south". One or two had brought their cars and offered to take me out. Austin Jones was a very careful driver, keeping his speed down and following the centre of the road. He envied my sleeping through the night as he had to get up every hour. Our bedroom at the front of the house overlooked the Great and Little Ormes and on one clear day I fancied I could see the Isle of Man. On most days I could make out tall buildings towards the Wirral and Liverpool.

One of the car owners wanted to impress me with a drive over Denbigh moor. I enjoyed the ride which included a stop in Llanrwst where I bought a local tourist book in Woolworths. The moor was good but I preferred the English Lake District. Best of all was a stop at the "marble church" at Bodelwyddan. Looking like a white iced wedding cake, the building really impressed me and there was a group of wartime graves outside of the Canadian crew of an RAF bomber. One Sunday my fellows asked me where I would like to visit and I chose Bodnant Gardens which they did not know. Unfortunately, the gates were locked and it seemed Bodnant did not open on Sundays.

Missing my one chance to see Bodnant while in North Wales was compensated for by a walk round Conwy, Telford's bridge and the town and a drive on the toll-road round the Great Orme. We stopped part-way round to look over the cliff edge to see Guillemots and Razorbills nesting. Rocks were bounding down the grassy bank above us from grazing sheep. We decided the sheep were kicking rocks at us. I enjoyed a walk on the pier at Llandudno where I learned that steamers had formerly ferried people to the Isle of Man. After that we walked on the beach at Rhos-on-Sea to visit the quaint St Trillo's chapel.

During my second week it became clear that I was there for two weeks only and this was the usual period. I complained to the management that I would not have agreed to leave home for a mere two weeks. The journey had been too much of an ordeal. Being unaccompanied and unable to stagger even to the toilet while on the move. They understood and must have discussed things with the management at Bocking. The result was that I was permitted to stay a further week plus a further £5 pocket money for that extra week. Every Monday morning when Dr Wainwright came to assess the new intake, I was also seeing him to my great benefit.

In answer to my question, Dr Wainwright told me he had experience of caring for post concussion patients both in and out of hospital. He was certainly right for me at that time. I heard later that the good Doctor had told the Convalescent Home management that my stay there was so beneficial to me that he had requested I be given another week there. This resulted in my being permitted to stay a fourth week plus a further £5 pocket money for that extra week also. I did not see Dr Wainwright again to thank him but I thanked God for the good Doctor and for all my many blessings.

The Convalescent Home was a pleasant enough place with a sizeable garden where we could walk or on warm days we sunbathed on the lawn. I remember lying on one of the lawns there and watching bees feeding on the wild white clover. The house had formerly been the home of a diamond merchant, perhaps not of gemstones but in connection with the nearby industrial diamond factory. These would not be sparklers but the kind of diamond we used for dressing our grinding wheels. A games room in the house was the previous owner's billiard room and it held the only fullsize billiard table in my experience. On my one journey with Austin Jones he took me past the industrial diamond factory.

We might walk down to Colwyn Bay town where I could put my pyjamas and underwear through the Launderette. So the £5 pocket money was useful there. Sometimes I walked in the opposite, inland, direction where there was waste ground with green woodpeckers feeding from anthills. Once I walked some distance further and found a gaunt grey church which notified itself as "The Cathedral of the Mountains". Had I been in better health, I could have requested transport to church on Sundays. The offer was available freely but I knew of no one accepting it and I was in no condition to benefit therefrom.

Memories of those four weeks will remain with me but they drew to a close and I had to leave North Wales and return to my native Essex. By contrast with the outward journey of which I remember every hour and many minutes, I remember nothing of my return journey. Back at home I could resume listening to Short Wave radio including Trans World Radio. It did me good to hear Pastor Dennis Paterson on the Live a New Life weekly broadcast on Wednesdays. I wrote to them at the announced address and we received an invitation to meet the Come Back To God Campaign Team at one of their Conferences.

I gathered that these Conferences had been held in various part of the country and in 1974 they would hold their final one at Mundesley on the north Norfolk coast. But this was still 1973 and I was not well enough to travel as far as Norfolk, quite apart from making the arrangements. Long before that I received a bitter blow. I was still hoping for and expecting a return to work some day for Samuel Courtauld at Bocking but the weekly visits by their Nurse came to an end. One week she brought my cards, unexpectedly terminating my employment.

Dr Wainwright of Colwyn Bay judging by his experience said he would expect my recovery from concussion to take between 18 months and two years. Now Courtauld's had cast me adrift after only six months. A fact I had to accept. But memories of my four special weeks in their Convalescent Home remained with me. I shall always be grateful for Courtauld's generosity. But for subsequent employment when I needed it, I would have to look elsewhere. For the present I remained close to young Alan's level and unemployable. And we both knew that he was better than me at some things.

While continuing to submit Sick Notes to Social Security I therefore had to continue requesting a doctors signature. One of the doctors objected to this arrangement and wanted me to go for rehabilitation. Mr Rose at the Social Security offices made arrangements for me to have a stay at Woodlee, the Employment Ministries IRU at Egham. The Industrial Rehabilitation

Unit appeared to be less a place for rehabilitation than for assessing the long-term unemployed. People who were expected to require a stay longer than two weeks were allowed a weekend at home. This happened in my case but while at home I caught a dose of influenza. Other residents suffered similarly. So my extended visit home was accepted with good will.

In all I had six weeks at the Egham Establishment. And once again I spent weekends with David and Christina as I did when they were in Canning Town. Christina had become Matron at a Children's home in Crondall, Hants and the Council at Woking or somewhere employed Dave. I could easily travel by bus between Egham and Farnham, which is not far from Crondall. I quite enjoyed my weekends at the Home in Crondall. But Lieut Stan Skelton had encouraged me to visit the Salvation Army in Egham where, he said, I would be welcomed by the Officer in charge. One Sunday morning therefore, I intended to go.

The road outside the Egham IRU was the A3 between London and Portsmouth. I waited at the bus stop until the time for church had passed. Always a busy route, on Sunday mornings the traffic was dense and barely moving. Not far from where I waited was a pedestrian entrance to Windsor Great Park with a footpath to the famous Savill Gardens. A gentle stroll to the nearby Valley Gardens was wonderful. Rhododendrons, azaleas and heathers were in bloom. Seats carved by chainsaw from large tree boles offered themselves and I sat in one in the Spring sunshine. An ideal situation for anyone in my condition and far better than any organised church. I sat there thanking and worshipping God as I absorbed the atmosphere.

Six weeks at Egham, plus a week at home with flu, had not restored me to the condition I needed to be in for full employment. The time came for my discharge and it became apparent that I was intended to have regular gym sessions as some others were having but they had omitted to inform me. At my final discharge I was told that my health had not permitted me to gain full benefit of being there. When better I should apply to go again. This in fact did occur after many years had passed.

But my condition was improving and back home I was taking notice of events around me. I learnt that the local WRVS were advertising for drivers for the Meals-on-Wheels service. Our boys Philip and Stephen enjoyed accompanying the Salvation Army officers delivering Meals-on-Wheels. Lieutenant Stan Skelton was encouraging and so I walked to the WRVS office which was not far away. I found that in asking for drivers they really meant car owners. But they had a small van which was used or borrowed by the District Council for the Wednesday Lunch Club. Meals for this were cooked at the School Kitchen in Manor Street and delivered to the Club at the nearby Community Centre.

From the WRVS office I was sent to see Mr John Kenny at Leahurst where the Community Services Department of the Council was based. Mr Kenny was pleased to accept me as a volunteer driver for the Wednesday Lunch Club and soon I was also driving for the Meals-on-Wheels service. This was in May 1974. The WRVS meals were then cooked at Black Notley Hospital and loaded into Hot-lock containers. I was loading the hot-locks into the van and delivering them to St Michael's Hospital where the Meals-on-Wheels people collected them for distribution around Bocking and Braintree. Even though unpaid, I had responsible duties on three days per week.

In addition to the Meals-on-Wheels on Tuesdays and Thursdays and the Lunch Club on Wednesdays, I was sometimes requested to take salvage clothing to Brand and Howes in Chelmsford. After these activities and helpful experience, I began to feel able to take on a proper job. I was helping Barbara by meeting Alan from his school in New Street. No other child came out of school as he did. Different versions of the Bible speak of going out leaping, or skipping out "as calves from the stall" (Malachi 4:2) and that is a picture of young Alan as he left St Michael's Primary School. Boundless reserve energy after his day in school.

An Application Form from the Education Department for full-time work did not help me to know where to turn for a reference. By then I knew many people who would have gladly given me a Reference but I was still muddle-headed and could think only of the Council officers at Leahurst. John Kenny may already have moved on but the two Welshmen, Alan Lomax and Bob Lumley remained longer. They advised me that as a Caretaker for the Education Department, I would be expected to perform work beyond my capabilities. Working off the ground, climbing ladders and suchlike work. If I waited, they would try to get a full time job for me. And this they did.

Whether the job they would arrange was any easier or more suitable for me than the one with the Education Department would have been, I did not know. But my work would be with the Community Services Department of the District Council and at first it would include driving the WRVS van on the accustomed three days. My immediate Supervisor would be Bob Lumley and he wanted me to start next day, a Thursday. To my muddled mind this seemed wrong and I could not agree to begin work on any day but a Monday. And we agreed to this.

But Lumley had a particular reason for me to be with him on the preceeding Thursday. His responsibilities included visiting all the various public buildings and halls with supplies. I agreed to accompany him in that but because my wish was to begin paid employment on a Monday, I went for the ride, rather than for pay. He took me to the Pavilion at the Cressing Road King George's Playing Fields. We went on to the halls at Silver End and Rivenhall. Then in Witham to Cross Road, Spring Lodge, Dengie Close and Forest Road. In time to come I was to take responsibilty for duties at a number of these public buildings. We also visited the Council Offices in Witham that day where I was introduced to the unforgettable Len Backler.

Council workers were so poorly paid that the weekly wage they could offer me was less than the benefit I received while recovering from severe post concussive syndrome. With a wife and three dependent children, I was of course receiving more than the minimum rate. Therefore, to make my work worthwhile, the Council Personnel Department agreed to pay me more than the going rate for manual workers. I began on the Monday morning 12th August 1974 working in the basement of Corner House, opposite the Town Hall. This was where the stock of ballot boxes were kept and I was busily stripping off red tape and sealing wax, checking padlocks and affixing the keys with fresh red tape.

Full time work for the Council would mean a cessation of my Benefit cheques posted from the Social Security offices in Panfield Lane, Braintree. All these bore a striking, even sinister, postmark, with a reproduction of a human head. They all carried the legend, *"I am your Countryman. Join with the mentally handicapped."* This had almost happened in my case. I was pretty useless for many jobs and the chronic vertigo which I can never shake off confirms the truth of what young Stephen pointed out once after we had walked to our home in Braintree. "Daddy can't walk straight" he said, which I realised was worth committing to memory. Both physically and mentally, you could say I'm a queer fish.

By this time I had booked to attend the final Conference of the Come Back To God Campaign at Mundesley in Norfolk. Some of the Community Services officers thought a bus service followed the Norfolk coast and that this would be our best route to Mundesley Holiday Camp. When the time came, Barbara, Alan and I bussed to Norwich where various bus routes ran in all directions. The one problem with this was when, in a rural hedge-lined lane, a speeding sports car drove into the side of our bus. The impact flattened the bus's exhaust pipe against the tyre, stopping its engine dead.

The sports car driver continued on his or her way but the bus driver could not restart his engine, so tightly was the pipe end closed. Somehow the driver made contact with his depot and all his passengers had to wait there until a spare bus arrived. We were actually nearing the end of our outward journey and might from there have contacted Mundesley Holiday Camp, if we had only known. In fact, we waited there till relief arrived. Picking and eating blackberries along the roadside helped to pass the time. Eventually we arrived at Mundesley where the bus took us to the windmill adjacent to the Holiday Camp.

We settled in and began getting to know some of the Campaign Team. The programme for the week was under the direction of Pastor Dennis Belsham – always known as Pastor Ben. One day as I walked on the sports field with Pastor Ben, a big rugby-playing chap, he said abruptly "You need healing". "Do I?" I replied, and told him I was willing to comply with whatever was decided. Over the years since first becoming acquainted with the Come Back To God Campaign, it has been apparent that their healing and deliverance ministry is conducted in a discreet and private manner. Unlike some in my experience who resemble a GP who might leave his office to doctor you in the Waiting Room, before an audience of other people.

Late one evening, at Pastor Ben's direction, I was taken by Terry Brinkley to an empty chalet, accompanied by a young man named Richard Hogarth. We sat in silence for some minutes until Terry informed me that God was telling him I had physical injuries, perhaps broken bones, in my left forearm and in the back of my neck. (This was before the Brinkley brothers were ordained.) I readily agreed that something was amiss in my arm or wrist but I knew of no trouble in my neck. Taking his cue from my answer, Terry, whom I now know as Pastor Terry ministered in prayer and gently explained that I might not notice any immediate change.

We were back in our home when I realised a healing change had taken place. I was in the bath and called Barbara to see that I had full use of my left wrist, demonstrating that I could now squeeze the bath sponge with my left hand. Which I had been unable to do for some time previously. With increasing activity I found there was in fact a problem in my neck which was causing me daily headaches. The only way I found to obtain relief was to stretch the back of my neck by holding my chin down. Not an easy thing to do continuously.

It was only some years later when at a Campaign Conference in Scotland that I mentioned the first healing of my wrist and requested further ministry for my neck. Praise God! I received the healing I so much needed and never again felt those troublesome headaches. Since the Campaign took over the old Mission Coast Home at Saltcoats, I have attended quite a number of holiday Conferences there and several times experienced deliverance as a touch from the hand of God. The first time I travelled there was quite an adventure in itself. For some years the Campaign supplied the Pastorate for a Mission Church at Laindon in south Essex.

The adventure began for me by staying overnight at my mother's in Brentwood. I had to be up early and ready to leave when my brother Peter came to take me to Laindon. Pete left me with the young Pastor – Philip something – and from his house we collected a Baptist couple for a hurried drive by minibus to Ealing. A luxury coach picked us up there with a good number from Ealing and Perivale. That was probably when we picked up two more outside Watford. The coach and driver stayed with us for a really enjoyable week in Ayrshire.

Other Campaign Conferences at Saltcoats have been less adventuresome but I have made the journey again by coach as well as by car and a few times by train. At least twice I travelled there by Air from Stanstead. Journeying in a jetliner built for paying passenger was vastly different to flying by the RAF Hastings of my last trip with the ROC. Thinking of these happy times I marvel that it began by listening to the Live a New Life weekly programmes on TWR. Sadly, these Campaign programmes have long since been discontinued. With more Supporters and greater finance, the broadcasts might have continued much longer. Even so, I greatly value my continuing contact with these Godly people I have come to know as friends.

My work for the Council Community Services Department increased. Besides driving for part of three days, I had to take responsibility for some of the Council-owned Public Buildings. The first of these was the former home of the Community Association and renamed by the new Braintree District Council as "Youth Hall". After witnessing the responsibilities of my brother David, I was sure that I would never choose to be a Caretaker. But in my new job with BDC I became the Youth Hall Caretaker/cleaner for a good part of the working week. A Committee of three Councillors, Tony Everard, Alan Millom and Bob Watson oversaw the Youth Club.

The hall recently vacated by the Community Association and now renamed Youth Hall was unlike any other Council building and many rules and regulations had to be disregarded to permit or allow the various functions. Its floor area and structure were both unlawful. Built during WW II for military dances and suchlike, it comprised merely a group of wooden huts. The regulations clearly stated that for such uses a Public Building had to be constructed of brick or stone and therefore fireproof. Its permitted occupancy numbers must have come from wartime functions, being greater even than that of The Institute and the emergency lighting by gas was unsuitable in a wooden building.

One other feature of the Youth Hall made it unique among the various BDC Public Buildings. Its heating came from a solid fuel boiler. With the other Council Buildings all heated by more modern means, I was the only Caretaker shovelling coke and boiler ashes and stoking the boiler both day and night. If they had realised it, my employers should have been grateful for my early training in my first job. For kindling I used to scrounge wooden boxes from the nearby Fine Fare Supermarket. Besides the Youth Club, regular functions using the Youth Hall were the Concert and Marching Band practicing on Thursday evenings and Bocking Brass on Sunday mornings.

All these things along with the Two JJs discotheque and Rock and Roll club, besides frequent Jumble sales meant that the Youth Hall was a very busy building. Not to mention its Caretaker/cleaner, still recovering from severe concussion. I found that my addled brain required as much sleep as an infant. I washed and polished the main floor which was of composition material, the kitchen and side hall and toilet/cloakrooms. Between cleaning and heating the building and supervising evening lettings, I used to go home to bed. Sleeping by night and part of the day used to occupy fourteen hours of each twentyfour. Greatly benefiting my recovering brain.

It was late one Saturday when Hazel Jarvis sent a message from The Institute where she was on duty for functions there. Poor Hazel had no one but me to call on when she was taken ill and had to go home by taxi. It would have been good if my employers had been as grateful to me as was Hazel. The Institute was the busiest of all the BDC Halls in Braintree, Halsted and Witham. On the occasions I have worked at Witham Public Hall or any other of the BDC buildings – including the Town Hall for Council Committee Meetings – the normal was for functions to be held singly. Whereas different rooms at The Institute might be hired for a number of functions concurrently.

From a large Social event down to a small private Birthday Party with Committee, Trade Union and Club meetings besides, I have had as many as five concurrent functions at The Institute during a single evening. And perhaps other events earlier in the day. My full time duties at The Institute were enough to satisfy any working man. But I missed driving the little Bedford van of the WRVS. The van was serviced by the Council at their depot in Hay Lane. Driving there for a pre-booked service one day, I parked the van with its wheels straddling the deep inspection pit. This seemed to be the obvious thing to do.

But the sight of all four van wheels on and over the edges of the pit when I left the driving seat was not to be repeated. My hair must have shown my alarm. To reverse the van when the time came, I chose to release the parking brake and allow the Fitter to push the vehicle from below. Too late I realised the inspection pit was intended for servicing Refuse Wagons, Dust Carts and similar HGVs. While still driving the WRVS van for BDC, I sometimes had the job of cleaning the Public Conveniences in Witham and Halsted. And of course I used the van when on duty for Sunday Schools or Blesma meetings in Witham.

This lifestyle must have been too good for me and eventually I was removed from regular work at The Institute and given charge of the failing Great Bradfords Hall two miles away. The chief difficulty there was the lack of public transport. The last bus to Braintree from Great Bradfords was no later than 7pm. This unhappy fact was reported to my superiors and the suggestion came to buy a bicycle. I ought to have considered and remembered that I had discontinued biking before leaving Lancashire. But I disregarded my own safety and began riding a bike to and from work after the buses had finished. Risktaking has shaped my life.

Another serious difficulty with which I had to contend at the Great Bradfords Hall was the awkward timing of lettings. These of course were not arranged for the convenience of Caretakers or cleaners. I was never consulted. To get full use and profitability of the building, all possible hirers were accomodated. This often meant that a late function on Saturday evening was followed next by a Mothers and Toddlers group on Monday morning. With no time between for such as floor cleaning. My instructions were that I could go there for cleaning on Sundays but that I would not be paid between midnight Saturday and starting time on Monday morning.

After washing and polishing the hall floor following one late disco I set out to cycle home well after midnight. That led to yet another concussion and hospitalisation. I remembered reaching the Railway St junction and heading for Bank St but the next thing I knew was regaining consciousness while sitting up vomiting into a kidney bowl. I would not have thought this possible but found I was in 'G' Ward at the old Chelmsford and Essex Hospital in New London Road. Prior to being found unconscious and bleeding in Clare Road, I had obviously cycled across town and almost home before some unknown hit-and-run driver overcame me. My bloodied raincoat was ruined.

While I remained unfit, a married couple were employed to do the work at Great Bradfords. I eventually restarted there but the job was never the same again. A cupboard I had taked there for my property had been broken into and items stolen. Five lightbulbs mistakenly supplied by Theobald who had taken on the work of supplying Caretakers and Cleaners were missing. In all that building only a single lightbulb was used, in the storeroom. All other lights were fluorescent strips so I had requested one bulb only. Theobald insisted on bringing me a box of six bulbs with the spares perhaps going to light the home of the mysterious married couple.

Braintree District Council began in April 1974 along with other local authorities and was still organising itself when I was employed the following August. I was told that I was a very small cog in a very big wheel and that I should be aware of internal vacancies and apply for advancement. Knowing that I was not caretaker material and feeling my abilities more suited to office duties, I tried to follow the advice I was given. But even speaking to the Chief Executive availed me nothing. Following my early retirement in May 1982, the Head of Community Services told me I would never be promoted as long as he was in charge.

While at BTR, I had joined the trade union of Municipal and General Workers which was recognised by both the rubber industry and by local authorities. Fortunately, I had decided to rejoin the Union and attend their meetings while with BDC. Rather than being a small cog in a big wheel, it seemed that menial duties or discharge were all I could expect. The MGW Union helped me to obtain a pension on grounds of permanent ill-health and I became a free man. Mr Riordan, the Personnel Officer told me he did not see it as retirement and he expected me to obtain another job although I could never again work for BDC.

My last duty for Braintree District Council was on 9th May 1982 and in September that year I signed on at the local college for the formal education I had missed. Part time attendance at the college in just a few years enabled me to obtain some 'O' levels and after these were discontinued I added two GCSEs. I enjoyed learning but my new knowledge was purely for pleasure. One part-time job came my way when the local factory of J. Mastenbroek advertised for part time secretarial help in their office. They were constructing large crawler-tracked land-drainage machines at the rate of one per calendar month.

Then Mastenbroek decided to build these one-per-month machines along with their other models at their Boston factory and to close the Braintree works. The men remaining on the shop floor were all skilled welders and fitters. They were readily found other jobs but it was less easy for me. But part-time secretarial work at the Mastenbroek works on Springwood Estate was not my final paid job. A uniquely different factory on the nearby Broomhills Estate needed a Cleaner. Vacuuming dog hairs from carpets was a big change for me from typing letters or answering the phone. And the delicate electronically controlled machines of GJ Barnes were vastly different to the heavy crawler-tracked machines for land-drainage.

The unique machines I could see being designed and constructed at this small Broomhills factory would automatically slice open a wooden tea chest, empty the contents, weigh and pack the tea into packets of loose tea or of bags ready for Supermarket shoppers. All untouched by hand. The same factory produced the drawings and all paperwork for buyers and prospective owners. Mr Gordon Barnes told me he was supplying another machine he designed to handle pistachio nuts. "As Jacob sent to Pharaoh", I reminded him. But perhaps not in fact to Pharaoh but to Joseph, Jacob's missing son. The variety I knew in my first job became a life long way.

While unemployed but still under retirement age, I was obliged to sign on for Jobseekers Allowance. This was when I remembered my six weeks spent at the Ministry Establishment "Woodlee", Egham. I recalled the advice I received there, to get fit and then to re-apply. My request to return was unwelcome and almost refused. Two other unemployed men from Braintree were being sent there and I was permitted to go with them. The place was modernised and the proceedures used had greatly changed in the intervening years. Everyone was assessed in one week. There are names for the different psychological tests we were given but we were not told their names or titles. Similar methods were used in an application for the prison service.

At the Egham IRU this second time we sat at desks in a classroom and our assessment was on papers. Some was with differing shapes and others about use of English language. Most of it has gone from my memory but I have a clear recollection of God's Holy Spirit helping me with one English expression. We were given a list of words and asked to give opposites. Voluble was one given word and I thought to write laconic as an opposite meaning. But before I wrote that down, I felt the Holy Spirit say "Put taciturn". I had never previously used this word but did so and felt happy about it. We were never given results of our work but told only what to do on returning home.

My assessment was completed by the Thursday. I received permission to return home at once but asked to be allowed to complete the week there. I spent time in the office enjoying Book-keeping on one of their Amstrad PCWs. The young lady psychologist advised me to apply for voluntary work in a hospital while continuing the Soon letter writing. She seemed quite interested in my letter writing for Soon, a Christian charity which was also voluntary. Another book could be filled with the friends I made overseas. All had completed a series of bible lesson courses in Easy English before I received their details.

Back home, I continued writing letters to many Christian friends overseas, some of whom have visited us in Braintree. Although deemed unfit to serve in the Armed Forces, my working life in three areas of Essex and more than four in Lancashire kept me reasonably fit. I could not avoid times as a Hospital Inpatient with surgery in at least six of the dozen hospitals where I had treatment. With outpatient check-ups besides, of course. Three motorcycles and four or five push-bikes kept me active and twenty-one glider flights added to my enjoyment. Not least was a flight on the London Eye or a memorable flight across Essex under a balloon. This last was to celebrate my 70th Birthday. The year-and-a-half delay in this event typified my life with episodes of ill health. But I survived.

It was being housebound following an emergency ankle operation that helped to delay my balloon flight so long. Many kind friends visited me and one or two female District Nurses were coming to change my dressings. As many as five of them were in my room together one time. One of them remembered my father from when she was a child. Another time a male Nurse came to remove adhesive strapping from my torso but I forestalled him. He arrived after I had eased the pack off my own ribs.

BIBLE READING

The Elim Sunday School rewarded our regular attendance usually with a book. One year Rex Nottage and I both decided to ask that we might receive a Bible as our prize. It was made clear that this would not signal the termination of our attendance. That was normally marked by the gift of an expensive Bible. Instead, they bought us cheaper pocket-sized bibles with limp leatherette covers. We had to take them with us each week, whether or not we read them. No one ever suggested that they were to be read. I was normally in church at both the morning and evening Meetings besides afternoon Sunday School.

All adult meetings of the church included a talk or sermon preceded by a brief reading from the bible. Such short readings always appeared insignificant compared with the talk which normally followed. With this in my background, I was surprised when one man recommended reading through the bible as you would any other book. He said you are not satisfied with reviews, commentaries and the thoughts of other readers of a book. You form your opinion through your own reading. This was after I began courting Barbara and her parent took me to hear this respected teacher. They suggested I question this man.

He could not answer my first question on his talk but remembered he had a bus to catch before moving away to chat with other people. I took my next opportunity to ask Pastor Harold Young about this new thought of reading God's word. He was all for it and told me that someone had read it all more than one hundred times. That was all I needed. I began to read my pocket-sized bible with the leatherette cover. Always restricting myself to stop after reading a full chapter; never having heard of a longer reading. But I persevered until reaching the end. I then began again but taking less time at the second attempt.

By then we were living in Preston and from the WEC Bookshop there, I bought another bible similar in appearance but this one included a concordance. After finishing this, I returned to the WEC Bookshop where Jack Hewitson recommended the RSV and sold me a hardback copy of this version. Years later I once read that blue RSV through within six months. I proceeded to acquire and devour other versions. In Braintree I bought a version of the Jerusalem Bible from Hannays, our local Bookshop. Following my second reading through that, I bought a limp cover copy of The Living Bible. I read through all my bibles at least twice.

My copy of the New International Version came by post from the Rochdale Bookshop of the Come Back To God Campaign. While I was reading that one, a Competition was announced from the Billy Graham Evangelistic Association which stipulated that the strangely titled Revised Authorised Version be used. I find that the so-called King James Version had never been officially authorised so why term its modern Revised Version so?

Learning that my friend Pastor Dennis Paterson used and recommended the American Standard Version for its use of italics for non-literal phrases, I made sure to add this to my library. These and other versions I read carefully through two or three times.

Besides these complete Holy Bibles, I have several copies of The New Testament beginning with a hardback illustrated edition from my childhood. In 1976 I bought a copy of The Translator's New Testament from The British and Foreign Bible Society. This special New Testament has been very interesting and helpful in studies.

The Daily Telegraph also helped. Each year certain people are asked to recommend their choice of a book for Christmas. One year, Enoch Powell wanted to be greedy and suggested two books. His first choice was a recent version of the Bible. And his second choice was of the William Tyndale translation of the Bible in modern spelling by David Daniell. I ordered first his New Testament and later the Old Testament besides. Excellent books.

HOSPITALS EXPERIENCED

Chelmsford and Essex
St John's (Chelmsford)
Broomfield (Chelmsford)
Essex County (Colchester)
Preston Royal Infirmary
Black Notley
Brentwood District
Harold Wood
Harefield (Middlesex)
Oldchurch (Romford)
St Michael's and William Julien Courtauld
[both at Braintree]

Lightning Source UK Ltd.
Milton Keynes UK

171572UK00001B/1/P